Graham Seal is a has published man topics, most recently *The Lingo: Listening to Australian English* and the *Encyclopedia of Folk Heroes*. He is also the author of *The Bare Fax*, a best-selling collection of Australian e-lore.

To Jen:

linking of you
in australia

~ Allison

GREAT AUSTRALIAN

URBAN MYTHS

REVISED EDITION

THE CANE TOAD HIGH

GRAHAM SEAL

■ HarperCollins Publishers

HarperCollins*Publishers*

First published in Australia by Angus & Robertson Publishers in 1995
This revised edition published in 2001
by HarperCollins*Publishers*
ABN 36 009 913 517
A member of the HarperCollins*Publishers* (Australia) Pty Limited Group
www.harpercollins.com.au

HarperCollins*Publishers*
25 Ryde Road, Pymble, Sydney NSW 2073, Australia
31 View Road, Glenfield, Auckland 10, New Zealand
77–85 Fulham Palace Road, London W6 8JB, United Kingdom
Hazelton Lanes, 55 Avenue Road, Suite 2900, Toronto, Ontario, M5R 3L2
and 1995 Markham Road, Scarborough, Ontario, M1B 5M8, Canada
10 East 53rd Street, New York NY 10022, USA

National Library of Australia Cataloguing-in-publication data:

Seal, Graham, 1950-.
    More urban myths: the canetoad high.
    ISBN 0 7322 6986 5.
    1. Urban folklore - Australia. 2. Anecdotes - Australia.
    3. Australia wit and humor. I. Title
398.20994

Cover illustration by Julian Chapple
Cover design by Luke Causby, HarperCollins Design Studio
Typeset in Sabon 10/13pt

Printed and bound in Australia by Griffin Press on 79gsm Bulky Paperback White

5 4 3 2 1   01 02 03 04

As well as friends, colleagues, family and those individuals named throughout the book — and some, who for their own protection are not — I would like to thank Maureen Seal, Jenna Seal, Kylie Seal, Gwenda Davey, Bill Scott, Phyl Lobl, Dave Hults and Carol Murphy.

Contents

INTRODUCTION: FOAFS, FACTOIDS AND MEMES

IT HAS BEEN SIX years since *Great Australian Urban Myths* or *Granny on the Roofrack*, as most people call it, was published. Since the mid–90s Australia, along with the rest of the world, has experienced an upsurge in the number, occurrence and sheer 'awfulness' of these supposedly true tales. Folklorists usually call them 'urban legends' or 'contemporary legends', though they are more widely known as 'urban myths' to the very large number of people who don't care to split hairs about the difference between a myth and a legend.

Whatever we wish to call them, there are some important reasons for the recent growth of these modern folktales. One of these is the eternal human urge to tell a good story even better than the last time. This is the 'one that got away' element; the fish that eluded the fisherman just gets bigger every time he retells the story.

Then there is the influence of the Internet, especially in the form of the World Wide Web and e-mail. The rapid development and penetration of these communication technologies has accelerated the spread of information, and misinformation, around the world. As there are virtually no controls over who or what goes on the net, much of the information transmitted is spurious or dubious at best. Urban legends thrive in this environment, especially as these latest forms of communication are remarkably like the oldest form, word of mouth, only bigger and faster.

A related factor in the upsurge of urban legends is that the phenomenon has become widely known. As a result of folklorists — notably American, Jan Brunvand and others such as Briton, Paul Smith — publicising their research in this field, journalists and others in the communication industries, including filmmakers, have become familiar with the genre and have in turn passed on their knowledge in the media. Journalists now refer routinely to urban legends or myths (though they are often still taken in by them). The popular BBC TV series 'The Vicar of Dibley' featured a number of urban legends in its nativity episode, clearly assuming viewers would know that the stories were 'factitious' urban legends. There has even been a major feature film titled *Urban Legend* (1998), with a sequel in 2000, as well as a number of lesser-known films that deliberately use urban legends in their plots and marketing strategies. At least one major European television documentary has been produced on the subject. As well, the general public have read many of the collections of legends that have come into the marketplace since Brunvand's *The Vanishing Hitchhiker* (1980).

'Familiarity breeds contempt', goes the proverb. As we become used to something it loses its novelty and we search for ways to make our tales more interesting than the 'old' versions. There are even a number of urban legend parodies in circulation — a sure sign of over-familiarisation. The result of all this is that old favourites like **Kid(ney)napping** become gradually more grotesque, and 'new' urban legends strive to attract attention by presenting even more bizarre or shocking events as 'true'.

FOAFS

Urban legends are usually defined as tales that are told as truth, yet when they are investigated cannot be verified. In this, they are closely related to another ancient form of folklore, rumour. But urban legends differ from rumours in that they have a definite narrative structure with a beginning, a middle and an ending; and, in that ending, they usually have an explicit or implicit moral or warning. So, the classic teenage terror tale of 'The Boyfriend's Death' or **The Head**, in which a girl's boyfriend is killed by an escaped maniac and she is rescued from the car on which the maniac is banging the boyfriend's severed head, is easily interpreted as a warning to young couples not to park in lonely spots. **The AIDS Coffin** story can be interpreted as a warning against unprotected sex with strangers, and so on.

Brief though these 'it happened to a friend-of-a-friend' or

'FOAF' stories are, they play upon some of our most common anxieties — the safety of our children, the threat of HIV infection, the randomness of accidents. Other legends congregate around cultural and psychological fault lines related to race, gender, technology, strangers, journeys, sex and crime. Urban legends exist because the things they deal with exist as part of the modern world.

However, many of them are not new. Some legends, and many of the elements that make up legends, can be traced back decades, centuries and even millennia. The basic situation of the modern legend usually known as **The Copulating Couple,** in which a man and woman are unable to disengage after sexual intercourse, is also found in the Greek tale of Aphrodite and Ares, who were magically bound together in their adultery by Aphrodite's angry husband, Hephaestus. The blood-spattered dog of **The Faithful Hound** was protecting his master's home and family during the Crusades and, almost certainly, long before.

Why are we still recycling and reworking these age-old motifs and themes? One answer is that the more things change, the more they stay the same. As technology becomes more sophisticated, we like to think we become more civilised — more rational and intelligent — as time goes on. Often we do, but underneath all the change and progress some fundamentals remain. These include concerns about the security of home and the family, suspicions of strangers and foreign places, uneasiness at new technological developments, an abiding fascination with sex — especially with its odd potential for embarrassment, the purity of the food we eat, and a miscellany of other worries.

It is human nature to want to talk about these things, even when they frighten us. But instead of addressing our fears directly, we work them out in story form. In the case of urban legends, these stories are brief and hence easily remembered; anonymous as befits large urban societies; and usually arresting — because we have become so accustomed to hyperbole and exaggeration that our attention cannot be caught by anything less than the bizarre or the grotesque, preferably both together.

In an earlier era we told each other tales about what happened to little girls who went into the woods alone. From the seventeenth century we transformed these chilling but useful tales of pre-industrial societies into a form suitable for the more refined and educated 'modern' society, and invented the 'fairy tale'. The young girl travelling alone through the woods, heroine of many ancient folktales, became the literary *Red Riding Hood*. She still had a narrow escape, but now it was with the help of the woodsman rather than her own cleverness and so the original folktale elements of sex, cannibalism and defecation were quietly forgotten. In the era of mass conflict, with genocide and the other horrors that regularly assail us either in person or through the mass media, there are no narrow escapes, no matter how romanticised. Urban legends — even the funny ones — almost always end badly for the individual or individuals involved. In their often gruesome or shocking details they reconnect us with the folktales of an earlier era and perform much the same service as a form of warning about what *might* happen, even if the events they recount never *did* happen — at least not to a friend's friend in the shopping centre in the next suburb some time last week — 'I think'.

Untrue though they generally are, urban legends and related forms of modern folk belief can be more than yarns we spin to each other over a beer or a cappuccino. Despite the supposed rationality of modern society, some of the nonsense carried in urban legends has been taken seriously by those in influential positions, and used against groups and individuals, usually with a devastating effect. Beliefs about Satanism have resulted in legal prosecutions and other forms of harassment that are no more than modern witch hunts. Australia experienced this in the 1980s with the Azaria Chamberlain case. Accusations of Satanic Ritual Abuse and related fantasies have resulted in serious miscarriages of justice in Australia, Britain, America and elsewhere.

As the sometimes unhappy consequences of modern mythology show, the elements that make up much urban legendry hardly ever die. They may go underground for years, decades, even centuries, but they only slumber beneath the surface, waiting to be shaken back into our consciousness by appropriate circumstances. There are many such examples in this collection, including the ever-present restaurant and food contamination tales, organ kidnaps as well as business and commercial rumours and legends.

But despite our increasingly sophisticated understanding of urban legends — our parodying them with books like this — most of us still believe many of the urban legends we hear or see. Are we all just gullible, or is there something about these tales that make us accept them at face value? This is the '64,000 dollar question' which most people who take a serious interest in urban legends would like to answer. Whatever the answer is, it has something to do with the relationship between lived experience and belief.

In February 1997, a water-bombing plane used for bushfire control crashed into a house in the Perth suburb of Bassendean. Fortunately no-one was killed or injured. The next day, a teacher at a local college was told that when the rescuers arrived at the scene of the crash they witnessed a strange sight. Wandering in a daze through the wreckage was a man dressed in full scuba diving outfit — wet suit, goggles, flippers, air tanks. The diver had been scooped out of the sea by the water-bombing plane as it refilled its tanks.

When the pilot realised the plane had a mechanical problem, the water was jettisoned near the crash site in an attempt to avert the crash. Of course, the scuba diver had been washed down to earth with the sea water. The teacher, who had some familiarity with urban legends, said to his colleague: 'You don't really believe that story, do you?' According to his report, the colleague was taken aback and replied that she had no reason to doubt its truth.

We do, though. This is a well-known urban legend that has been collected in many parts of the world. Usually the scuba diver gets dumped onto the forest fire along with the scooped up sea water and is found — sometimes dead, sometimes alive — in a vulcanised state when the fire has burned out.

Like most urban legends, this one could just be true, though most would probably reject it as nonsense. But in the circumstances described, there was an actual event that allowed someone to dredge up the story from memory and to attach it to that event. The teacher was simply spreading the news along the chain, as were dozens, perhaps hundreds of others. The previous event of the water-bombing plane crash was sufficient to set up in her mind a preliminary fact that verified the urban legend. This is frequently the case with urban legends. Some circumstance or set of circumstances that are verified seem to invoke relevant urban legends and provide an appropriate context in which they can spread. A number of examples of this process will be found in the following pages, especially in relation to **The Great Kidney Panic of '98**.

We don't necessarily need facts to predispose us to accept urban legends. Belief, especially in the form of prejudice, will do just as well, if not better. So a good many urban legends are credible because they turn on perceptions we have, often unconsciously, about 'others'. These can be people from other countries or ethnicities, they can be those with a different sexual orientation, or even the opposite gender. Prejudices of this kind, for instance, produce and perpetuate stories about Asian restaurants serving poodles with the noodles, a great favourite in Australia and in most other western nations. Likewise, a fear of homosexuality, held by some Australians, motivates legends about AIDS.

As the scuba diver anecdote highlights, an increasingly experienced difficulty in these legend-savvy times involves how to tell someone that the story they have just told you, and which they clearly believe to be true, is a load of, well, bullshit. This can be an especially tricky piece of interpersonal communication. If it isn't handled well you can flatten a social moment and severely strain a friendship. There are a number of possible approaches you could take.

One is simply to say nothing. Just smile and nod your head agreeably at what you are being told, smug in the knowledge that you know it's just an urban legend. The other extreme is to inform the teller straight-out that what they have just told you is only male bovine ordure. If either of these alternatives is unpalatable, try the PPQ approach recommended in American folklorist Jan Brunvand's 1993 urban legend book, *The Baby Train*.

Readers of Brunvand's previous books had experienced extremely negative reactions when trying to debunk legends being told to them and wrote to the professor asking for his advice. He recommended the 'Polite Persistent Questioning' technique. As the story unfolds and it becomes obvious to you that this is an urban legend, politely ask the speaker questions about the credibility of the events described. So, if you were being told the yarn about the scuba diver, for instance, you might say something like: 'I didn't think that the scoop on water-bombing planes could go that deeply into the water.' When the teller gets to the bit about the diver being conveniently dumped along with the water as the pilot tried to save the plane, you might say something like: 'You'd think the diver would be dead, or at least badly injured, wouldn't you? How lucky can you be!'

As Brunvand says, the idea is not to confront the storyteller with his or her gullibility — after all, it can happen to any of us, even folklorists (see **Going by the Numbers**) — but to create an atmosphere of innocent doubt that might also encourage others present to ask questions. When it becomes obvious that the storyteller has been taken in it is advisable to give them an 'out' by saying something like: 'Oh yes, I remember where I heard something like that before. Didn't I read about it in a book by Jan Harold Brunvand called ...' Brunvand then goes on to recommend that all present should be directed towards bookshops stocking his collections. Give it a try. But don't complain to me if it backfires. (You might consider directing great numbers of people to copies of my book, too!)

Another useful technique in urban legend-busting, and one that insulates you from any potential flak from your believing friends, is to direct legend-mongers to one of the urban legend websites listed in the section **More About Urban Legends** at the back of this book. You can do it by e-mail, if you're really worried.

But seriously, debunking a story in which someone has invested their belief is a dangerous undertaking. None of us appreciates having our myths trodden on, especially face-to-face.

Other useful debunking approaches will be found at various points throughout this book and also in the final chapter **Don't Be Myth-Taken**. There you will find some reasonably detailed suggestions about protecting yourself and others from the ravages of urban legendry. If that's all a bit much, here's a condensed pocket urban legend-busting kit that can be very helpful.

URBAN LEGEND DETECTION KIT

Pocket Version

1. SOURCE
Ask for the source of the information.
2. VARIATION
If you hear or read the story again, from whatever source, do any of the details vary, even a little?
3. EXAGGERATION
Does there seem to be an element of exaggeration in the telling?
4. YUK FACTOR
Is it unusually high?
5. SENSE
Is it logical and rational?
6. STORY
Does it have a story-like structure?
7. FOAFs
Does it feature named protagonists or is it the usual 'friend-of-a-friend'?
8. MORAL
Does there seem to be some kind of moral or warning attached to the tale?

These eight simple questions should help you bust most of the urban legends that come your way. Don't leave home without it.

Since *Granny on the Roofrack* was published, quite a few people have contacted me with 'new' or 'different' versions of legends they have heard and, usually, passed on. The many press and TV interviews and especially radio talkback sessions that I have done on this subject since then have also provided me with a good deal of further information about 'old' legends as well as 'new' ones from all over the country.

I have also continued to collect and research these naggingly persistent narratives in Australia, overseas and through the World Wide Web. The results are contained in this book, which updates many of the 'old' legends included in the earlier book — some of which seem to have now achieved 'classic' status — and pins down plenty of 'new' ones. In some cases I have retained the legends included in the earlier book with little or no updating, mainly because these are particular favourites or because they are still in circulation without much change, at least as far as I am aware. Urban legendry is, thank goodness, far from being an exact science. For the most part the legends have been arranged in different categories, in order to highlight the ways in which these modern myths operate, and the consequences they can have.

FACTOIDS AND MEMES

I have also included some stories that are not strictly 'urban legends', but which operate in very similar ways and trade on our credibility, usually to our disadvantage. These include such things as the rapidly proliferating Internet and e-mail hoaxes, scams and get-rich-quick schemes, as well as rumours and other kinds of hearsay. A good catch-all term for these scraps of mis- and dis-information is 'factoids', a term apparently coined by the American novelist Norman Mailer to describe the scandalous gossip that American newspapers published and continue to publish about Marilyn Monroe. Two American social psychologists, A. Pratkanis and E. Aronson, proposed the extended use of this term in their 1992 book *Age of Propaganda: The Everyday Use and Abuse of Persuasion*. As with urban legends the folk saying 'forewarned is forearmed' is appropriate here.

A recently developed approach to understanding the transmission of ideas, catchy tunes, chain letters and just about any other kind of cultural information is called 'memetics'. This approach stems from the best-selling book about evolutionary biology by Richard Dawkins published in 1976. Titled *The Selfish Gene*, Dawkins, almost as an afterthought, applied the idea of genes carrying biological information through organic communities to the transmission of ideas through culture. He called these nodules of meaning 'memes'. The theory is that just as human genes transmit genetic information from one body to the next via reproduction, so memes transmit cultural survival information through society by oral transmission, through the media and, more recently, through the Internet. One of Dawkins' examples of a meme was a catchy pop tune that seems to appeal to just about everyone at more or less the same time. He and a colleague later applied the meme theory in a more serious way to study the chain letter, a form of modern folklore, seeing these endlessly recirculating combinations of threat and promise as an example of memetic transmission.

This is an interesting idea that has attracted a lot of discussion in recent years, with people applying it to all sorts of cultural forms, including urban legends. Like most grand explanatory theories it is suggestive in explaining the 'how' of such things, though still does not get to the bottom of 'why' things happen the way they do. In the context of urban legends it could be argued that because the information contained in them is of great importance — they warn us about things that might happen — they have a cultural imperative to survive and spread, just like 'the selfish gene' of Dawkins's book title. However, as the information contained in urban legends is only apparently true, it could be just as logically argued that these stories distort our ability to operate effectively and comfortably in our society. This is not to say that the memetic approach to urban legends is without value, simply that it is beyond the scope of this book to discuss in the required depth. Interested readers will find some references to memetics at the back of the book.

Given the international distribution of FOAFs and factoids, you might wonder what is especially Australian about them? Australians like to think of their myths as primarily those of the bush. We have a great deal of our historical imagination and emotional nationalism invested in images of pioneering, overlanding, the gold rushes, bushrangers and the elements of the great Australian legend powerfully expressed by writers like Henry Lawson and 'Banjo' Paterson, and artists like Frederick McCubbin and Tom Roberts. So pervasive are these images that it is easy to forget the vast majority of Australians live in cities and surrounding suburbs, and have done so since at least the early twentieth century.

As well as the lore and legendry of the bush, we have developed an extensive body of urban mythology. This includes a good deal of humour, folk speech, photocopy lore and urban legends. Not only is this material circulated by word of mouth, it is increasingly spread by electronic means, especially via the photocopier, the World Wide Web, e-mail and the facsimile machine, as demonstrated in my 1996 book *The Bare Fax*. While these are relatively recent forms of technology we find that what amuses us, appals or inspires us has not changed a great deal. We still cut down tall poppies, dislike authority, and expend a good deal of energy deflating the pomposities and absurdities of politicians, political correctness and officialdom.

This collection of urban legends demonstrates these truths in abundance, and then some. Even though many of the themes and concerns of Australian urban lore are shared with other parts of the world, our selection, adaptation and treatment of these relate closely to our traditions of irreverence, independence and the colloquial. As with folk traditions elsewhere, ours are much concerned with themes of everyday life, including work, sex, leisure, travel, the worrying and the unexplained. While these expressions are in most cases very different from the earlier traditions of old bush songs and swagmen's yarns, they still relate to the ideas — accurate or otherwise — we have about ourselves as a people and so are an important part of contemporary Australian folklife.

So, no matter what we call them, how we arrange them or how we analyse these anecdotes of our age, the redbacks are still multiplying in the dreadlocks, hatchets are still being found in the back seat of the family car, and poor old Granny is still up on that roofrack — out there, somewhere.

2

SEX 'N' STUFF

S EX, IN ALL ITS VARIETY and absurdity, is a perennial theme of modern legendry. Some of the best — and the worst — legends are accommodated in this large category of humour and angst which ranges from the amusing to the outrageous, taking in the ridiculous, the painful and the prejudiced along the way.

A favourite topic of legends around and about sex involves people caught in embarrassing sexual, or apparently sexual situations, as in the stories about **The Piggybacking Baby-sitters** and **The X-rated Honeymoon**.

Closely related to embarrassment is surprise, especially when the surprise is of the type described in the stories gathered together under that heading. Here are elaborations on the subject of surprise parties, the odd uses of peanut butter, and mistaken identity.

The spurned lover is a near-universal theme of folklore, old and new. In its modern forms it can involve the creative use of super glue and alfalfa, as well as the unusual pricing of expensive cars.

The sex act, or more exactly acts, provide the opportunity for the expression of both humour and prejudice in urban legends. The gentle amusement of **The Blackout Babies** is counterpointed by the alarming possibilities of lovemaking in automobiles, and the homophobic tensions still being generated by misconceptions about the AIDS virus.

In this selection of sexual peccadilloes, anxieties and plain bad luck, much has been left out, including such delights as the cling-wrap condoms, and the aphrodisiac properties of various soft drinks, lollies and other foods. Did you hear about the bloke who won Lotto, then gleefully informed his wife that he had been screwing her sister for years, and that she was welcome to the house and car? Later he discovered that he had not won after all. Oops.

Despite these absences, the legends that fill the following pages provide a reasonably representative sampling of the current sexual concerns in Australian urban legendry. Given the universality of sex, and the creativity of humans, it is certain that reality is far stranger than many of the tales told here. But don't let that put you off.

PROCREATING AND RECREATING

THE BLACKOUT BABIES

There was a strange surge in the number of babies born around the same time in a particular region. The explanation for this was that there was a power blackout nine months earlier. This meant that people were not able to spend the night in front of the TV, and had to amuse themselves in more traditional ways.

This is more or less how I first heard the story in New South Wales back in the 1960s. It was not new then and, in one version or another, has been recorded throughout Australia and around the world.

Instead of a power blackout, the reason for the nocturnal high jinks is often the regular and noisy arrival of the night train. Folklorist Bill Scott has a superb version of this one in his *Pelicans and Chihuahuas* (1996) given to him by an anonymous fat cat at Queanbeyan Leagues Club in 1978. His version had an appropriate bureaucratic setting.

The census office was puzzling over the figures of the recent census held in the New South Wales north coast town of Kyogle. They couldn't work out why this place had a birth rate

three times the national average. An officer was sent to investigate, and found the school crammed with kids, and even a special new wing added to the maternity hospital. After a few days, the officer worked it out.

The Kyogle mail train used to pass through town about 4.30 every morning, blowing its whistle at the level crossing on the north side of town, waking everyone up. Just as they were dosing off again, the train would cross the crossing on the south side of town and blow its whistle again. By then, just about everyone in town was wide awake. It was too early to get up, but ...

Bill Scott found another version of this legend while reading a book about an English village, set around the turn of the century. He later discovered the story was also told in the town where he lives, Warwick. And it is so well known in one particular South African town that the local offspring are known far and wide as 'train babies'.

American folklorist Jan Brunvand titled a whole book about urban legends *The Baby Train* (1993). He remembered being told a similar story in Michigan during the 1950s — the train arrived at 5am there. He also quotes South African urban legendist Arthur Goldstuck — author of a number of South African urban legend collections — with further details of the story in that part of the world. Brunvand includes references to the power blackout versions similar to the one I heard, including the New York City blackout of 1965 and a story refuting a possible version of the legend after the 1990 San Francisco Bay Area earthquake.

THE COPULATING COUPLE

A young man and woman who had been going out together for some time had reached a stage in their relationship where sex was often an urgent matter. On one particular day, as neither of them had a place of their own and they couldn't afford a hotel room, they decided to go for a drive. They found a suitably private spot at the edge of the city and began making love.

Unfortunately, their passionate contortions in the confined space of the car caused some sort of physical reaction and they became locked in congress. Unable to escape each other, they were forced to lie there, crying out for help until someone finally came to their assistance. Incredulous, and trying to stifle his laughter, their saviour drove them to the nearest hospital where the deeply embarrassed couple were surgically separated.

Also known as 'The Stuck Couple', this legend is popular in hospitals, where it may be told as a kind of initiation rite for new casualty ward or operating theatre nurses. One ex-nurse told me she had first heard it in this manner while she was an apprehensive trainee in the 1960s.

English writer Rodney Dale included a stuck couple legend in his 1978 book *The Tumour in the Whale*. I collected a variation of **The Copulating Couple** in Sydney, in October 1986. In this version the male's foot becomes jammed in the car's ashtray and the couple are placed in the humiliating position of having to call out for passers-by to extricate them. Sometimes this story is told with the man simply putting his back out while the couple are in action.

Versions of this one, which has been traced to ancient Greek mythology — though without the car — are still in active circulation. Whatever the version, the implied moral is pretty clear, as it is in a number of sex-in-a-motor-vehicle legends, such as the old one in which a young woman was secretly given 'Spanish Fly' or some other aphrodisiac by her boyfriend. Usually this took place at a drive-in cinema. The young woman becomes so sexually aroused that she cannot wait for her beau to join her and so engages in frenzied intercourse with the gear stick of the car, with fatal results. While this legend is little heard today, if at all, it does resonate with the current cycle of 'date rape' stories mentioned later in this chapter.

The following fable also involves the often disastrous combination of sex and automobiles. In this case the results are not necessarily fatal, though perhaps even worse.

A BIG CRUNCH IN THE MOUTH

Richard Snedden of Forbes wrote in with a grisly variation of **The Copulating Couple**. Richard remembers first hearing this one at university in the early 1970s.

A young man and woman were killed when their car crashed into a tree. He had been driving and she had been committing fellatio on him. The force of the crash made her bite the top of his penis off, and it was still in her mouth when the ambulance arrived.

Ouch! An obvious warning about inappropriate behaviour in the car, this gruesome sex accident legend tends to stick in the mind. It certainly stayed with Richard, who had a vivid recollection of it after more than twenty years.

GETTING YOUR OWN BACK

THE WEDDING PHOTOS

No, not the usual shots of blissful newlyweds and proud mums and dads. This is a tale of revenge before the marriage is even consummated.

At a wedding reception it was the groom's turn to say a few words. He got up and asked the guests to look under their seats. Puzzled, they did as they were asked, and found taped beneath the chairs photographs of the bride in an extremely compromising position with the best man. In the stunned silence, the groom then announced to everyone that he was leaving his brand-new wife, and that the cost of the wedding, borne by his parents, was his revenge on them (for what, was not specified).

This was said to have happened 'in America or somewhere'.

Popular in various forms in America during the mid–80s and into the 90s, this one has been heard quite a bit in Australia in the late 90s and well into 2000. Sometimes the photographic evidence is taped to the base of the plates on the festive table. Often there is no revenge motive and there may be a fight between bride and groom. Usually the reception continues. After all, what's a wedding without a decent blue of some sort?

This legend also exists in a version told from the opposite point of view.

It comes the bride's turn to say a few words of thanks to the assembled company. She works her way through the lengthy list of parents, minister, friends, family and finally comes to the Maid of Honour. 'I'd like to thank my Maid of Honour most of all,' she coos. 'I especially want to thank her for sleeping with the groom last night.' She then stalks out, leaving the guests to recover and party on or not, as they prefer.

THE DIVORCEE'S REVENGE

The following sexual revenge legend comes from the latter end of the marital journey.

'One Saturday morning a couple of years ago a friend rang me up out of the blue. He said he'd be 'round my place in a couple of minutes to tell me something.

'He comes around. When he got to my place he said, "Jeez, I just looked in the paper and there is an advertisement for a Mercedes Benz, the latest model, going for $50."

"'What's the problem?" I said. "How can it be going that cheap?"

"'This man's getting divorced," he said. "His wife wants to divorce him and his wife wants half of everything he's got. What he has to do is sell the car really cheap so his wife doesn't get much money."

'So I said, "Show me where it is." He wasn't sure he could find the ad, so I really didn't see it. But a lot of other people said they saw it.'

This is a slightly less macabre version of **The Death Car** (included in Chapter 4) and so, perhaps, more believable. It is often called 'The Philanderer's Porsche', but any expensive car may be substituted, as in this version told by a seventeen-year-old in 1988.

The Divorcee's Revenge was probably hairy when it was first documented by British folklorists in the late 1940s. A reader of American urban legend expert Jan Brunvand's books sent him a version so old that the car was a $20 Packard. The car, and the price, varies from country to country. In Britain it is a £5 Rolls, in America a $50 Porsche. The car may be a Cadillac, Volvo, Kharmann Ghia, Jaguar, BMW or other expensive auto, but no matter how cheap it is, it doesn't exist.

This example gives a good insight into how quickly modern legends can be transmitted and how they can be easily altered to suit all kinds of circumstances. The teller is quite happy to pass on the story as 'true' even though, as he says, he did not see the advertisement in the paper — but a lot of other people did.

Another well-told evergreen also involves the theme of marital disharmony and some fairly solid revenge.

THE CONCRETE CAR

A man who made his living as the driver of a ready-mix concrete truck was a very jealous type. He constantly suspected his good-looking wife of having affairs with other men while he was away. One day he went off to work as usual, but realised he had forgotten to take his lunch with him. He decided to drive home and pick up his lunch, but when he arrived he found a brand-new, shiny, red Porsche convertible parked in the driveway with the top down. He could see his wife sitting on the lounge with a well-dressed young bloke.

His suspicions confirmed and his jealousy inflamed, the man manoeuvred his concrete truck into position and dumped the entire load on the Porsche. Feeling very pleased with himself, he drove off.

When he returned home that evening, ready to have it out with his wife, she greeted him in tears, pointing at the very solid pile in the driveway. 'I won the Porsche in an Art Union,' she sobbed. 'A young man had just delivered it, when some bastard filled it up with concrete.'

Some versions of this popular yarn, also known as 'The Ready-mix Revenge', have the wife actually in bed with the young bloke and the truckie simply getting his solid cement revenge. I prefer the irony of the version above. Whatever version, **The Concrete Car** is told all over Australia (often located on the Gold Coast) and has been collected around the world. It was particularly popular throughout Europe in the early 1970s, and American folklorists have unearthed versions of it going back to the 1940s. Some suggestions claim that it may have originated in the 1920s, when a story about a garbo dumping his load into a Stutz Bearcat was reportedly told in America.

An American study of this legend highlights another aspect of the relationship between legends and reality. Louie W. Attebery embarked on a quest to find the origins of **The Concrete Car** legend. Like many folklorists and legend sleuths before, Attebery thought the legend had finally been sourced to an incident reported in a Denver, Colorado newspaper as long ago as 1960. Someone filled a 1946 DeSoto car with concrete — though the motive of revenge was not a factor in this actual event. Alas, other research showed that the legend had been in active circulation in the state of Texas at least four months earlier. It seems possible in this case, and in a number of other documented instances, that the existence of the story gave an individual the idea of carrying out actions similar to those described in the legend. Folklorists call this process by which fantasy becomes fact 'ostension' or an 'ostensive action'. There is another example of ostension in the section titled **The Minister's Telecard** in Chapter 6.

Ostension is the other side of the coin from the often-asked question 'Have the events described in urban legends ever actually happened?' The following colourful tale of a young woman's revenge is most unlikely ever to have taken place, but it's not hard to imagine someone being angry enough to give it a try.

THE ALFALFA REVENGE

A young woman had a torrid relationship with her boyfriend. Although the bloke had made an offer of marriage, the girlfriend discovered that he'd been sleeping with another woman all the time that he'd been wooing her.

Shortly after she made this discovery, the man took off on a week's holiday and, still simmering with rage, the betrayed girlfriend decided to take her revenge while he was away. She still had the key to his flat, and so she let herself in the day after he'd left.

Saturating the carpets, bed, furniture, curtains and everything else in the place with water, she then threw handfuls of alfalfa seeds all around the flat. When the faithless lover returned he found his carpet, curtains, furniture and, of course, his bed, smothered in a thick layer of green alfalfa.

This is another version of stories about lovers' revenge that reveals an inventive turn of mind. It belongs to a small but memorable group of legends dealing with the revenge of the slighted lover. These include those mentioned above, and one in which a woman discovers her husband is having an affair while away on a supposed long business trip. She packs her bags and dials the number of a very distant and expensive time and temperature information service, and leaves the receiver off the hook for her husband to find on his return some weeks later.

The Superglue Revenge is another popular legend of this type.

THE SUPERGLUE REVENGE

A woman came home from work unusually early, went into the bedroom to change and found her husband asleep with his beautiful blonde secretary. The wife's first impulse was to scratch both their eyes out but, having thought of a better revenge, she restrained her anger.

Instead, she went into the kitchen and found a tube of superglue. Returning to the bedroom, where the lovers were still asleep, the wife carefully superglued her husband's penis to his leg, emptying the whole tube onto the penis for good measure. She then left the house.

Soon afterwards, the husband woke up. Still sleepy, he wasn't aware of what had happened until he went to the bathroom and tried to pee. He quickly realised what had been done, and his secretary had to take him to hospital, where his penis was surgically separated from his leg.

In some versions of the story the husband's penis is amputated rather than just separated from his leg.

This revenge legend originated soon after the introduction of superglue to the commercial market in the 1980s. Its believability is greatly assisted by the fact that there were numerous superglue accidents which required surgery. Whether or not these were all 'accidents' is arguable. At the time, there were also many other stories in circulation about the prank of squeezing superglue onto the toilet seat. Due to incidents such as these — accidental or otherwise — the various forms of superglue on the market today seem to be formulated less disastrously for human skin and human relations. This legend has declined in popularity accordingly.

What is it about sex and revenge? The two seem to go together in urban legends as well as sex and the element of surprise — or perhaps that should be shock.

SHOCKING SURPRISES

THE SURPRISE PARTY

A married man worked in an office with a beautiful female secretary. On his birthday the secretary invited the man over to her place for a drink and dinner. Hardly able to believe his luck, the man quickly accepted and after work they drove to the secretary's flat.

Inside, she told the man to make himself comfortable while she went into the other room, saying she would be back in a minute or two. Anticipating a night of passion, the man undressed and waited naked, complete with an enormous erection. Suddenly, the secretary opened the double doors into the lounge room to reveal the man's wife, children, friends and co-workers all chorusing 'Surprise, surprise!'

Surprise and embarrassment are the joint themes of **The Surprise Party**, as it is usually known. For excruciating embarrassment, compare this one with **A Fart in the Dark** (Chapter 3) and **The Peanut Butter Surprise** later in this chapter.

American folklorists have made quite a study of this tale and its variations. They have found early tellings of it in the 1920s, and in the March 1997 *Reader's Digest* it turned up in the guise of a true story — an incident that really happened to the ex-boss of a reader.

In Australia, it is more usually told as a joke or humorous yarn (a fabrication) than as a contemporary legend (apparent 'truth'). According to legend scholar Jan Brunvand, it is more usually encountered in the United States as a legend. This may point to some significant differences in attitudes towards sex and nudity between the two countries, with Australians possibly being a little more relaxed about these matters than Americans. Versions of **The Surprise Party** are often circulated in printed form as a piece of photocopy lore.

The following verbatim item is a related 'shocking surprise story' — sometimes told as a joke, sometimes passed around in printed form.

AN EVEN BIGGER SURPRISE

DO NOT UNFOLD BOTTOM FOLD OR READ THE LAST LINE OF THE STORY OR YOU WILL KILL THE POINT.

There was this business executive who decided he needed a little rest from his daily routine, so he decided to take his pretty young secretary to a motel and spend the day.

So he rented a very nice motel room and they spent the day drinking, going to bed, having lunch, more drinking, back to bed again, etc. On the way home he was thinking about what in the world he would tell his wife if she insisted on having a 'party' tonight. He drove up the driveway of his home and sure enough, there was the wife at the door, well arrayed in a pretty gown and negligee, with his pipe, slippers and a cool drink.

She led him into the house with all the sweetness she possessed, to his favourite chair. He thought, 'Boy, this is going to lead to something.' They sat back and relaxed, sipping their drinks and talking. Suddenly she stated that she had forgotten something in the bedroom, got up and said she would be right back.

He thought, 'Oh, boy, here it comes.' As soon as she left, he jumped up, unzipped his trousers, pulled out 'Jasper' and started to beat and whip it around, trying to get some life into it, but nothing happened. It didn't help a bit. He heard her returning, so he stuffed 'Jasper' back into his pants and zipped them up and sat down and sighed.

They continued their conversation. Then she asked him if he would care for another drink. He replied that he would. So off she went to the kitchen to fix it.

He jumped up immediately, opened his pants again, out with 'Jasper' ... up and down ... around and around ... back and forth. All this was with much more vigour than before, but to no avail — he would just have to tell her that he was too tired for fun and games tonight.

She returned with their drinks, sat down and said, 'Dear, I have the most wonderful surprise for you and I know you will be perfectly delighted.'

He thought, 'Sure I will,' then said, 'Well, what is it?'

She answered with a silly smile, 'Guess what ... WE ARE ON CANDID CAMERA!'

This was circulating amongst nurses in the Blue Mountains area of New South Wales in 1983, and was not new then. It is an example of 'photocopy lore', another popular form of contemporary folk tradition, a selection of which can be found in my 1996 collection of photocopy, fax and e-mail-lore, *The Bare Fax*.

THE PEANUT BUTTER SURPRISE

A middle-aged woman who lived alone with her large pet dog had a birthday coming up, and her workmates decided to organise a surprise party at her home. The surprise would involve all of them sneaking into her house during the early evening. They were rather worried about the woman's dog barking and giving the game away, but decided to give it a go anyway.

The workmates all met in the woman's backyard at the appointed time and very quietly and carefully sneaked into the two-storey house. The dog was nowhere to be seen. Great. Now they were sure that they'd really give her a surprise.

They couldn't find the woman on the ground floor of the house, but there was a faint noise and a chink of light coming from one of the upstairs bedrooms. Ever so quietly, the little group of workmates crept up the stairs towards the half-opened bedroom door. They reached the landing, edged up to the bedroom door and threw it open, yelling 'Surprise, surprise' and 'Happy Birthday'.

They froze in a state of shock. The woman was lying stark naked on the bed, covered from head to toe in peanut butter which her pet dog was licking off her.

The connection between the woman's job and what happens in the story is consistent in all the versions. This very recent modern legend seems to be a development of 'The Surpriser Surprised'. It was on the Internet as early as 1994 and was also being told in Sydney later that year. Since then, this repellent tale has grown apace and spread (sorry) far and wide.

SURPRISE IN THE SHOWER

A man brought a workmate home one night to get ready for a function. 'You can have the first shower,' he generously offered his guest. 'I'm going down to the laundry to find some clean clothes to wear.'

The woman of the house returned home and went straight upstairs. Assuming that the person taking a shower was her husband, she reached in and playfully tweaked his genitals, before going back downstairs. In the laundry she finds her husband rifling through the washing and, horrified, realises her embarrassing mistake.

Like many urban legends, **Surprise in the Shower** has been around forever, and its variations are endless. It was a favourite of *Post* magazine, humour books and cartoonists. Sometimes the surprised showerer is the local minister, sometimes it is the man's boss. Always it gets a laugh.

In other versions, the wife mistakenly tweaks the genitals of the next-door neighbour, whose face is hidden as he works beneath his car, or of a plumber whose face is obscured as he plumbs beneath the kitchen sink. Alternatively, the man may have left his fly open and the wife, incorrectly assuming that the man is her husband, considerately and lovingly zips it up for him.

As with many urban legends, this one has also developed another twist. The man under the sink or beneath the car is so surprised by the sudden attention to his flies or genitalia that he jerks his head up, and smashes it into the sink or the car. This gives him a severe concussion and he has to be rushed to hospital.

This hilariously unfunny ending is similar to one that often extends the agony of **The Exploding Dunny** (Chapter 3).

[SERIOUS EMBARRASSMENTS]

THE PIGGYBACKING BABY-SITTERS

Out of the blue, a young engaged couple are suddenly asked to baby-sit for friends who'd been called away to an urgent family crisis. It was the young woman's birthday, but she and her fiancé were only too pleased to help out, knowing that after the children had gone to sleep they would have the house to themselves.

When the kids were safely tucked up in bed, the couple went upstairs to the bedroom, stripped off and began making love. Suddenly, they heard a noise downstairs.

'What's that?' asked the fiancé, alarmed. Then the young woman remembered: her friend told her that she had left the washing machine running and had asked her to switch it off when she heard it stop. 'It must have been the washing machine finishing,' she replied. 'I'd better switch it off at the power point or it might blow up.'

Reluctantly, she got up to go downstairs. In a mischievous mood, her fiancé suggested that, as they were alone in the house and the kids were fast asleep, they could whip downstairs in the nude. 'Here. I'll give you a piggyback,' he offered naughtily.

'Why not?' the young woman said, laughing. Still naked, she climbed up on her nude fiancé's shoulders. Just as they reached the bottom of the staircase, the lights came on. There before them were the owners of the house, the parents of the young woman, her fiancé's parents and all their friends shouting, 'Surprise! Happy birthday!'

I first heard **The Piggybacking Baby-sitters** from an American in the late 1980s, but it was certainly well known in Australia by then and has been with us ever since.

American versions were recorded as far back as the late 1950s, and folklorists there have done a good deal of research on this legend and its many variants, all of which deal with the theme of embarrassed nudity. In some versions of the story — mainly those of an earlier vintage — the young man is so mortified that he drops the girl, grabs his clothes and rushes off into the night, sometimes joining the army or the navy. The girl is often said to have collapsed from shock and shame, to have subsequently lost her mind and been locked up in an asylum.

THE X-RATED HONEYMOON

A couple of young newlyweds spent their first married night at a motel and had a wonderful sexual experience, in which the full range of possibilities was explored and enjoyed. For their first anniversary, the couple decided to return to the same motel to relive the experience. But before making love, they decided to watch an erotic video on the motel's

inhouse system. They were horrified to discover that the video was a secretly filmed record of their first night of lovemaking a year before.

This is one for those contemplating marriage! The fable is an update of the old story and the old fear of the string beneath the honeymoon bed that is connected to a bell in the guests' lounge. Moral: don't assume privacy when the premises are beyond your control, especially when *you* might be out of control.

I thought this one might be too old-hat to last beyond the mid–90s, but it still turns up on the Internet in the 'noughties'. Recent versions include the very modern elaboration that the couple was so happy at the way they had performed on the video that they tried to order a copy of the tape from the hotel.

THE NAKED CARAVANNER

A married couple took a caravanning holiday in the Outback. The heat was oppressive and the woman needed to rest. She decided to climb into the caravan while her husband drove on to the next town, hundreds of kilometres away.

It was so hot inside the van that the wife stripped down to her briefs and went to sleep. After a while she was woken by a loud bang — a blown tyre on the driver's side front wheel. Her husband swore and dragged out the jack and spare to fix the flat. Wanting to take a pee, and as there was no-one and nothing in sight in any direction, the woman, still in her underwear, climbed out of the van and squatted in the scrub beside the highway. The husband finished changing the wheel

and, not realising that his wife had left the van, got back in the car and roared off into the distance, leaving her near-naked beside the road.

Fortunately, a bikie came by after a few minutes. The embarrassed but desperate wife, flagged him down and asked him to chase after her husband with the caravan. The obliging bikie agreed, so she hopped on behind him and they roared off in chase.

They caught up with the caravan but couldn't attract the husband's attention, so the bikie decided to overtake and wave the husband down. As they sped past, the husband, seeing his wife in only her briefs on the back of the motorcycle, was so shocked that he ran the car off the road and was killed in the smash.

Fear of being caught nude, or in an otherwise embarrassing situation, is the theme of a number of contemporary fables, such as **A Fart in the Dark** and **The Surprise Party**.

This is pretty much how the most commonly encountered version of this tale goes in Australia, but American variations usually have the male and female roles reversed. I first heard this story told in Australia around 1986 and it was certainly around for a good while before then. It was collected in New South Wales as early as 1978 by Bill Scott, and was known in Perth in the mid–1980s. An Adrienne Eccles of Unley, South Australia, sent a good version to Jan Brunvand, which he published in his 1993 book *The Baby Train*. In the South Aussie version the action takes place on the conveniently located Nullarbor Plain and it happened to 'a friend's uncle and aunt'. Fair dinkum.

[FUN FOR SOME]

FIZZY COLON

A nurse was on night duty one evening when an emergency case was rushed into the theatre. The doctors and nurses had to perform an operation to extract a foreign object from a male patient's rectum. When the operation was over, the medical staff, previously intent on the other end of the patient's anatomy, realised it was a well-known celebrity.

In these versions of the tale, the foreign object is generally of the inert variety — a soft drink bottle being a recent favourite. There are various other renditions of this one involving a female celebrity allegedly enjoying an affair with a well-known male celebrity and who has a soft drink bottle (various brands are mentioned) removed from her vagina.

Early British versions of this one — minus the celebrity — were noted by Rodney Dale in his *The Tumour in the Whale* (1978). One of these told how a homosexual male was taken to hospital with a small pineapple juice bottle stuck in an inappropriate position. At first, the doctor could not work out how to extract the bottle without breaking it. Eventually, he took a wire coat hanger, shaped it into a corkscrew formation, and inserted it into the neck of the bottle — which was, fortunately, facing the right way round for this strategy to succeed. He then filled the bottle with plaster of Paris. When the plaster set, he was able to safely extract the offending item. As they cleaned up afterwards, the young student nurse in attendance asked wonderingly, 'However did he manage to swallow it in the first place?'

A closely related anecdote involves a young man with a length of thick-walled rubber tubing inserted rectally. According to the story, the hospital sold tickets for the operation. Only a local anaesthetic was used, and the patient enjoyed himself greatly.

Dale also tells the tale he heard during his National Service training, presumably during the 1950s, about an unpleasant second lieutenant who was something of a hypochondriac. This combination made him extremely unpopular with the patients in the military hospital. One day a patient from another officers' ward put on a white jacket and strode purposefully up to the second lieutenant's bed, ordering him to turn over and prepare for a rectal inspection. Thinking that the medicos had finally realised how ill he really was and sent a new specialist, the second lieutenant gladly obliged. The 'specialist' then slipped a previously greased daffodil into the second lieutenant's rectum and disappeared, leaving the patient in this richly deserved position.

BACKFIRE!

In May 1999 came a new twist to this particular cluster of legends from an article purporting to be from the *LA Times*. It told of a terrifying saga of gerbilling that had backfired. Two homosexuals named Eric and his partner Kiki were 'felching' with their pet gerbil named Raggot. Eric had popped Raggot into Kiki's rectum via a strategically placed cardboard tube. When Kiki declared he had experienced enough pleasure for the moment, Eric tried to retrieve

Raggot, but the poor little critter had become stuck inside. Thinking that he might be able to attract Raggot out with a light, Eric struck a match and placed it at the larger end of the cardboard tube. The hospital spokesman described what happened next at a hushed press conference:

'The match ignited a pocket of intestinal gas and a flame shot out of the tubing, igniting Eric's hair and severely burning his face. It also set fire to the gerbil's fur and whiskers which in turn ignited a larger pocket of gas further up the intestine, propelling the rodent out like a cannonball. Eric suffered second-degree burns and a broken nose from the impact of the gerbil, while Kiki suffered first- and second-degree burns to his anus and lower intestinal tract.'

Well, this one's got the lot, so to speak. To find a more complete example of an urban legend you would have to go very far indeed.

FULL UP

'I heard that in the 1970s, a famous English rock star had to be rushed to hospital to have his "stomach pumped" because he had so much semen in his stomach. I didn't think much of it until the period circa 1986–91 when the same story surfaced in reference to Freddie Mercury.'

So writes Richard Snedden, rural urban legendist from Forbes in New South Wales. This celebrity sex legend is also often attached to male rock stars. Richard's description of the legend gives a nice illustration of how legends survive the generations. The same basic, probably unfounded, circumstances are easily battened onto the latest pop icon, generation after generation.

Some American versions of this legend do not involve well-known celebrities, but focus instead on the female leaders of cheer-squads, apparently the objects of much adolescent male lust.

[NOT SO MUCH FUN]

FRIENDLY AND GAY

A young man was plied with alcohol or drugs by a friendly male to the point where he passed out. The next morning, he woke up with a sore anus, having been homosexually raped by the generous man while in a state of inebriation.

This is the kernel of a well-travelled and oft-told tale. Australian versions have been collected by Bill Scott, one dating back to the mid–1940s from the Royal Australian Navy, in which Scott served.

Jan Brunvand notes similarities between Scott's versions and one given by the noted sexual and geographical adventurer Sir Richard Burton (no, not that one) in his 1886 edition of *The Book of the Thousand and One Nights*. Brunvand has also identified other versions in American armed forces tradition and university student lore. In these stories the alcohol has usually become a stupefying drug such as ether or chloroform. In his 1999 tome, *Too Good to be True: The Colossal Book of Urban Legends*, Brunvand notes that this story was widespread in American student populations during the early 1990s.

Since then and into the 'noughties', the homosexual orientation of this legend seems to have swapped into the heterosexual. It is possible that there is a connection between these homophobic legends and the more recent stories of 'date rape', usually featuring a stupefying drug — originally Rohypnol ('Roofies' or 'Rowies' in folk speech), more recently the even more sinister and hard-to-detect GHB, short for gamma hydroxybutyrate — being smuggled into the drink of the victim at a nightclub or hotel.

One motif shared by both the homosexual and heterosexual date rape stories is that the victims, male or female, are often too embarrassed to report the incident to the police.

THE AIDS COFFIN

A girl became romantically involved with a visiting American sailor. They had a wonderful time, going to nightclubs, shows and, of course, to bed, but eventually it had to end as the sailor's ship headed off to ocean duty and other ports.

A few weeks after the tearful farewell, the girl was overjoyed when she received a small package in the mail from the sailor. She opened it excitedly, but was rather surprised to find a

small coffin inside, accompanied by a note. Puzzled, she removed the note from the coffin. 'How does it feel to know you have AIDS?' it read.

Many modern legends are communal responses to topical issues and problems. The AIDS virus and reactions to it provide a good example of this process in action, and this horrible little story is a version of a widely spun yarn that trades on the fear of deliberate HIV infection. It was doing the rounds in Perth (with the usual variations) where visiting American sailors are a frequent occurrence, in early March 1990. At virtually the same time the British *Sun* newspaper (on 6 March) reported that a group of Spanish playboys with AIDS had dedicated themselves to infecting visiting female British tourists. They had given two girls farewell gifts that turned out to be small wooden coffins containing the message 'Welcome to the death club. Now you've got AIDS'.

Since then this one has continued to appal us, despite attempts to educate and enlighten the general public about the realities of HIV infection. It is closely related to another AIDS legend, usually known as 'AIDS Mary', 'AIDS Harry' or 'Welcome to the World of AIDS', which has been widely reported throughout the world and in Australia from the mid to late 1980s. To see how elements of this legend have combined with another popular tale, see **Kid(ney)napping** and **The Great Kidney Panic of '98** in Chapter 5.

AIDS MARY

A man picked up a girl at a pub and they went to his home and indulged in intercourse without using a condom. In the

morning the man woke to find that he was alone. As he was getting up he discovered a card beside the bed with these words written on it: 'Welcome to the AIDS club'.

Other versions of this tale have the man waking up to discover, scrawled in lipstick on the bathroom mirror, 'Welcome to the world of AIDS', and often signed 'AIDS Mary'. This legend stems from the belief that there is an HIV-infected woman roaming around the country, seducing or propositioning young men in order to infect them, in revenge for her own illness. (There was, in fact, a woman called 'Typhoid Mary' who was arrested in New York in 1915 for, it was believed, deliberately spreading typhoid.)

The panic element is clear enough in this frightening tale. There have been, and probably still are, HIV-infected individuals who knowingly spread the virus. Although there are undoubtedly very few of these people, the wildfire spread of this legend since the late 1980s suggests how disposed we are to believe such actions are commonplace. Fears about sexually transmitted disease are hardly new, however, and it has been suggested that this legend may have been around in the nineteenth century, when syphilis was viewed with the same sort of fear as AIDS is today.

THE ORIGINS OF AIDS

Given the hysteria the disease has generated, it is not surprising that AIDS-lore is characterised by some bizarre assertions and beliefs. These include the well-known story that it was an invention of the CIA or the KGB that went horribly wrong and escaped the test tube by various methods. There are shades of Frankenstein in this one. Other 'where AIDS came from' stories involve monkeys, Africa, Haiti — even the English writer George Orwell (the author of *Animal Farm* and *Nineteen Eighty-Four*), who died of tuberculosis in 1950. In contemporary legends, AIDS has been said to derive from almost anything and anywhere 'different'.

In 2000, tests on monkey DNA for proof that the AIDS virus had begun there were inconclusive, undoubtedly giving legends of this sort another boost. Listen out for them around your way.

AIDS MEMOIR

Dear Sir,

I have just received the AIDS leaflet and would like to apply straightaway for AIDS. I have been on the dole for the past five years and have been living off the family allowance and every other state aid I could get. It now seems I will get aid for sex.

It's a pity AIDS didn't come sooner since I've got fifteen kids. Will there be any back payments? Your leaflet says the more sex I have the more chance I have of getting AIDS. The wife is not too keen these days, but since the government is now paying for all the sex we can have, we can't let a chance like this slip by. You also state that I can get AIDS from a blood transfusion. I will go to the hospital to see if I can have one.

Will the AIDS I get from the hospital be deducted from the AIDS I get from you? I am a firm believer in getting all the AIDS I can. Why didn't someone think of this before? We deserve all the help we can get. Do I get paid every time or in instalments?

Yours faithfully.

Just to establish that there is a lighter side to modern myths about AIDS, this is a piece of photocopy-lore that surfaced in Sydney in the *Weekend Australian* in June 1987. It was not new then and has been circulating ever since. This example parodies the 'AIDS memoir' title and is, allegedly, a reply to a Department of Health and Social Security leaflet explaining AIDS.

This genre is widespread and includes letters supposedly written to insurance offices describing automobile accidents with such lines as 'The guy was all over the road. I had to swerve a number of times before I hit him'. Another favourite of this kind are the extracts from letters sent to the Social Security or other welfare agencies, including 'Milk is needed for the baby. Father is unable to supply it'. And 'My son has been unable to attend school. He had diarrhoea through a hole in his shoe', and so on. There are also versions that purport to be the absurdities that students actually wrote in an examination circulating through the teaching profession. These and other examples can be found in my 1996 collection of photocopy-lore, *The Bare Fax*.

As up-to-date as we might think such material is, like most folklore, it can be traced back quite a long way. There are 1930s printed versions of the welfare letter in America, and I have a copy of a similar Australian letter in my own collection that appeared in print during the 1920s.

3

HORRORS — ASSORTED

RECENT FILMS LIKE *Urban Legend*, its sequel *The Final Cut*, and a host of lesser-known movies have all emphasised the horror element of modern mythology. It is certainly hard to avoid and provides us with an ever-changing menu of gory, grisly and just plain gross tales. Popular subjects of horror legends include family pets, bodily mutilations, serious embarrassments, awful accidents and infestations of the body's external areas, or worse.

The number and variety of horrible things that can happen to us and those we love — including animals — is worryingly large. Cats can be cooked and otherwise disposed of, babies can be microwaved, and brains can be eaten by earwigs. Bikies can be decapitated, rabbits exploded, and the ashes of the beloved dead unknowingly consumed by still-living family members. And even worse things can happen.

Attempted explanations for the popularity of these unpleasant stories are also numerous. Some have argued that they reflect our repressed fears about our security and safety in the increasingly alienating experience of modern living. Others take a psychological approach and see stories about bodily mutilations and the like as evidence of individual emotional problems. No doubt there is some validity in both these interpretations.

While many of these tales are truly horrific, there is also room for humour. Horrible embarrassments and even accidents can be uproariously funny, especially when they happen to someone else. There is no shortage of contemporary folklore on these themes of excruciating humiliation, especially those involving sex and explosive bodily functions.

Altogether, the variety and awfulness of these terrible tales suggests that many of us are less than comfortable with the realities of living in the early twenty-first century, and choose to express these insecurities in untrue, but nevertheless widely believed, urban legends of horror.

[THINGS TO DO WITH PETS]

PET MEAT

'A neighbour bought a pet chihuahua for $200 and took it home in a box. She put the box on the sofa and went out to the kitchen. While she was out of the room her cat ate the dog!

It must have thought the chihuahua was a rat! She ran over to see us just after it happened, and she was smiling. When we asked her what was funny she laughed and said her cat had just eaten a gourmet meal!'

This story was told in Perth in 1987 by a medical student who'd heard it at a Christmas party the year before. An article in the Perth *Sunday Times* of 14 November 1993 claimed the story was first heard in Australia at the Queanbeyan Leagues Club 'as a certain fact', in 1987.

Folklorist Bill Scott collected a good meaty version from Jindabyne, New South Wales, as early as 1983. According to the version he heard, the chihuahua was eaten in Canberra, but there are other variations of this gory pet story. In one, the little dog is scooped up as a snack by a hungry, low-flying bird of prey. (See also **The Baby-napping Bird** in Chapter 5.) In another, a woman's husband, jealous of the affection his wife is lavishing on the chihuahua, buys the biggest, fiercest cat he can find in the hope — soon realised — that the cat will mistake the pet dog for a mouse and gobble it up.

PRESSED CHIHUAHUA

A woman owned a pet chihuahua that she loved dearly. She pampered it in every way, feeding it choice tidbits, lovingly grooming its fur and generally treating it better than she would a human being. The animal even had a special chair of its own, covered with fine, expensive material.

One day the woman hosted a tea party. All her friends were there, dressed to the nines. One of the best-dressed and most refined female guests was grossly overweight, and after eating more cake than she should have, the hefty guest looked around for somewhere to sit. Her eyes immediately fell on the chihuahua's seat and, without another glance, she waddled across the room and sat down. Unfortunately, the much-loved little pet was on its chair, sleeping peacefully. Instant pressed chihuahua!

Pressed Chihuahua is an expression of the malice and jealousy that humans feel when canines get better treatment than they. Though it is worth noting that in most versions of the story an overweight woman rather than a fat bloke blots out the poor chihuahua's life of luxury. A couple of Queensland versions were collected by Ron Edwards in 1988–89, and almost everyone seems to have heard of this happening, somewhere, sometime.

DOG'S DINNER

A well-to-do French couple visited Hong Kong (or China or somewhere) and went to a local restaurant with their pet poodle. They asked the waiter for a meal for their dog, as well as for themselves, but there was a bit of a language barrier. Finally they sorted it out and the waiter took the dog out to the kitchen to look after it. Later, their meal was brought out to them and when they uncovered the dish they found the dog.

Contamination stories are related to another hoary modern myth — the Oriental delight in cooking and eating cats and dogs. Beliefs, rumours and legends with this theme are legion. Whenever a pet cat or dog goes missing in Australia it is inevitably suggested by someone that the owner check the local Chinese restaurant.

This well-known Chinese restaurant story is set many places — frequently overseas, especially Hong Kong, Singapore or Malaysia. It was reported in Zurich by Reuters news service as early as 1971. A Scandinavian version features Paris, with a rat in the dinner instead of a dog. In one of his collections of yarns, *Fred's Crab*, Ron Edwards quotes a version collected in Queensland in 1988. This locates the restaurant in not-very-exotic Adelaide and identifies the dog as a chihuahua.

The cooking of dogs and cats by Chinese cooks is an old theme in Australian folklore and was treated in verse in 1888 by James Brunton Stephens in *My Other Chinese Cook*. It is still a widespread belief in Australia that Chinese, Vietnamese, Cambodian and other such restaurants cook dogs and cats, usually picked up from the local area, but this doesn't seem to stop Australians from dining at these places. Perhaps this is an indication that we don't always believe what we say?

The most recent development of this legend appeared on the San Fernando Valley Folklore Society urban legends website in early 2000.

An urban legend trading on this theme involves a couple visiting Hong Kong or 'somewhere in Asia' from Switzerland, England or America. According to the story, the couple visited a restaurant with their pet dog, usually a chihuahua or one of the smaller breeds, and asked for a meal. The waiter had trouble understanding them but eventually picked up the pet dog and took it to the kitchen where the couple assumed the man was going to feed it. After some time he returned with a

covered plate. Upon taking the lid off the couple found their pet dog, cooked and served with bamboo shoots and other garnishes — sometimes on a bed of rice, sometimes with an apple or orange in its mouth. The couple usually suffer a nervous breakdown and return home immediately.

This one, in all its florid variations, is an example of the large category of food contamination legends, more of which you can find — if you're game — in Chapter 4.

BUNNY BUSINESS

The family dog came bounding into the backyard one day carrying the corpse of the next-door neighbour's pet rabbit in its jaws. Horrified, Mum took the dead rabbit from the dog, shampooed it, blow-dried it with the hair dryer and sneaked into the neighbour's backyard to put the now fluffy corpse back into its hutch.

Next morning, there was a scream from the neighbour's yard and the family ran next door to see what was the matter. The neighbour was gibbering and pointing at her bouffant dead rabbit in terror.

'I expect the poor thing died of a heart attack,' Dad suggested hopefully.

At last able to get words out, the woman shrieked, 'But I buried Snuggles yesterday!' and then fainted.

We are left to wonder what the end result of this touching little tale might have been. Did the embarrassed family revive the shocked neighbour, trying to explain and apologise, while cursing the dog? Why do we bother to tell such a trivial tale? Most of us hope to live in reasonable harmony with our neighbours, often in high-density residential areas where even small differences may become major conflicts. Even when we try to do the right thing in the hope that 'what they don't know won't hurt them', the potential is always there for our actions to have disastrous consequences. Similar to **The Dinner Party,** and related to the **The Resurrected Cat, Bunny Business** is told around the world.

It had another outing in *The Australian* of 3 September 1997, starring an Alsatian called Zeus and a bunny named Fluffy. The neighbour doesn't faint in this one. Instead, he is simply perplexed and thinks that someone has been playing some kind of sick joke on the family.

THE CAT IN THE BAG

A Perth woman had to go shopping but her cat had died, so she put it in her handbag with the intention of disposing of the body while she was out. As she was walking down the Hay Street Mall her handbag was stolen by a fat woman. The grieving pet owner chased the thief, but lost her in the crowd. Later, she came across a group of people standing around the same fat woman, who was lying on the ground. She must have opened the bag, seen the cat and collapsed from the shock.

This odd but persistent tale is often set in a shopping centre or department store and is frequently called 'The Dead Cat in the Package' because sometimes the woman has the corpse in a box or packet rather than her handbag. The story given here is how the tale was heard in Western

Australia in the early 1970s. It was still circulating there — and just about everywhere else — ever since.

The Cat in the Bag is one of the most widespread and long-lived of contemporary legends. It continually turns up in newspapers, has been treated by fiction writers in short-story form and appears in the autobiography of American humorist Alexander King, *May This House be Safe from Tigers* (1960), in which he implies, that the incident actually happened to him in the 1920s. When I published a short article on 'Mall Stories' in the May 1994 edition of the *Independent Monthly*, I included mention of The Cat in the Bag. In a subsequent issue a correspondent replied that he had read King's book and that King reported the incident as fact. The story, through such means, continues to be circulated and so given increasing credibility.

The tale's continuing appeal is probably due to its mugging or shoplifting theme. Both forms of robbery have become an unfortunately accepted part of modern living, and to have the culprit open his or her booty and collapse is a most satisfying scenario for many people. The Cat in the Bag has become so well known that it is now frequently heard as a favourite Christmas-time shopping story in America, Britain and Australia. During Christmas 1994, an American Internet user inquired of the world at large, 'Has anyone heard or read the urban myth about the dead cat in the shopping bag so far this Christmas season? This is the first time in several years I haven't been told as gospel truth that it happened to a friend of a friend's friend ... '

Bill Scott included a version of this legend in his 1996 book *Pelicans and Chihuahuas*. The dead cat turned up again in an article in *The Australian* in September 1997. The ending of this story involved the poor woman finding a leg of pork in her bag instead of the poor moggy. A case of letting the cat out of the bag?

POOR MOGGY!

A man was late for work and was driving very fast — too fast. As he rocketed down a side street he ran over a cat. Despite being late he decided to do the right thing, so he stopped the car and rushed over to the cat lying at the side of the road. It had pretty well had it, and was barely breathing, so he decided that the best thing to do was to put the moggy out of its misery.

After having a quick look around to see that no-one was watching, the man picked up half a house brick from the nearest front yard and smashed the cat's head in. Then, picking it up carefully by the tail, he dropped the corpse in a rubbish bin.

Soon, as he continued recklessly on his way to work, he was pulled over by the cops, but they didn't want him for speeding. It seemed that a woman had reported that a man answering his description had bashed her cat to death while it snoozed in the sun beside the road.

'Yes,' said the man, 'but I'd run the bloody thing down. It was just about dead. I only helped it along.'

While the man was telling his story to one policeman, the other copper checked out his car and beckoned the man around to the front.

'Did you hit the cat with the front of your car, sir?' asked the second policeman.

'Of course I did,' replied the man. 'What do you think?'

'Take a look at your front bumper, please sir.' The man bent down and there, squashed on the bumper, were the remains of a cat, very similar in size and colour to the one whose head he'd bashed in.

Another mistaken identity yarn. Poor moggy! Even though this story is not set in the workplace, it is usually told about a bloke hurrying to work, or a job interview. Or, the luckless moggy murderer is simply driving home too fast after finishing work, as in the version of the story printed in *The Australian* newspaper on 3 September 1997.

It has similarities with another story, in which a man gets very drunk but manages to drive home and park the car in the driveway, before collapsing on the living room couch. He is woken early in the morning by the screams of his wife. She had gone out to bring in the newspaper and found the mangled body of a seven-year-old girl wedged onto the grille.

Another cat legend provides a little light relief.

MAG WHEELS

A keen do-it-yourselfer came up with a great way to allow the family cat to get in through the kitty door, without being followed in by every other cat in the street. He fixed an industrial magnet to the door, negative pole out, and attached another to the cat's collar with the positive pole out. As the cat came close to the door, the positive pole repelled the negative pole, and the door opened like magic. The clever handyman also fitted a latch that kept the door closed after the moggy had entered.

All seemed to be going well, until one day the cat was nowhere to be found. The family frantically went searching up and down the street until they eventually found the cat. It was held to a car hubcap by the magnet on its collar, helplessly mewing.

I expect to soon hear of an elaboration of this one — just as the relieved cat owners find their pet, the car drives off with the poor moggy still magnetised to the hubcap.

Gives the term 'mag wheels' a whole new meaning.

THE COOKED CAT

A woman washed her cat, and put it in the microwave oven to dry it out. The cat cooked on the inside, swelled, and blew up.

This version of a very widespread legend was told by a man in 1987 in Western Australia. The tale continues to pop up every now and again, and has been around in one version or another for a very long time. Sometimes it is a small dog that gets the treatment. Whichever species is unfortunate enough to suffer this dreadful fate, the same story was being told about gas and electric ovens in the pre-microwave era.

According to Rodney Dale's *The Tumour in the Whale* (1978), cats, usually black, were being spun dry, cleansed in washing machines, frozen in fridges and cooked in ovens at least as early as the 1970s. But we had to wait for the invention of the microwave oven for the really macabre version, known as 'The Stoned Baby-sitter' or **The Baby in the Microwave**.

BODY PARTS – MUTILATIONS AND THE LIKE

THE BABY IN THE MICROWAVE

Requiring a baby-sitter at short notice one night, a couple hired a local man. They knew that he had a reputation as an LSD user, but they were unable to get anyone else who could do the job at such short notice. Despite their misgivings, they set off for the evening, having left the young man detailed instructions on what to do.

Sometime later, being concerned about the young man's reputation, the woman decided to ring home to check that everything was okay. 'How's it all going?' she asked anxiously.

'Fine,' the baby-sitter said brightly. 'I've just stuffed the turkey and put it in the microwave.'

The woman immediately panicked — as there was no turkey to be stuffed. Rushing home, the parents found the baby-sitter in a befuddled state. He had mistaken the baby for a turkey, seasoned it and placed it in the microwave.

Sometimes the parents get there just in time. Usually they don't. Known around the world for decades (in earlier versions it was the oven instead of the microwave) as **The Baby in the Microwave**, it trades on the fear of strangers, the vulnerability of babies and the neglect of parents who allow unsuitable people to mind their child. The story is reminiscent of the fairy tale of 'Hansel and Gretel', in which the old hag plans to cook the children in her dinner pot, and the message of both tales is much the same.

Jan Brunvand has done a considerable amount of research on this story and the closely related **The Cooked Cat**, the results of which are published in his recent book of urban legend studies, *The Truth Never Stands in the Way of a Good Story* (2000).

THE HEAD

At dusk one night a young couple were parked in their car on a deserted track. The radio was playing appropriately romantic music, while the youngsters kissed and cuddled. Suddenly, the music was interrupted by a newsflash warning that a dangerous maniac had escaped from a local asylum. Then they heard a strange noise outside.

The boy decided to investigate, telling the girl to lock the doors until his return. As the night turned pitch dark she waited and waited, becoming increasingly terrified when her boyfriend did not return. The silence was broken by a loud noise outside the car, followed by a thumping sound on the roof. Thump, thump, thump. By now she was petrified with fear.

Soon afterwards, bright lights glared into the car and the girl heard an amplified voice. 'This is the police. Get out of the car and walk towards the light. Don't turn around under any circumstances.'

Despite her fear, the girl managed to get out of the car and began walking towards the police lights. But she could not resist the temptation to look behind her. She turned to see the

grisly sight of the escaped maniac perched on the roof of the car banging the severed head of the boyfriend up and down — 'thump, thump, thump'.

The macabre story of **The Head** is well known throughout the world, and was used with good effect in the Australian film *Malcolm*. Especially popular among adolescents, this legend is very clearly a cautionary tale and one that has been told around Australia since at least the mid-1970s. Sometimes, however, the horrors of this story are too much to contemplate so close to home and the events are located far away — in America, Britain or elsewhere.

We tend to think of this as a very contemporary story, but many of its elements are of considerable age. Youthful lovemaking is nothing new and the girl looking back, despite the warning not to do so, is straight out of the Old Testament tale of Lot's wife being turned into a pillar of salt. The story also has a classical parallel in the tale of Orpheus and Eurydice. The ritualistic 'thump, thump, thump' is an ancient element of western folklore, in which things generally occur in threes. Versions of the tale have also been reported in Japan, and its essential ingredients have been traced back to 1949 in the United States. The wide spread of the legend and its horrific aspects have made it the subject of considerable research and analysis by folklorists and other scholars around the world.

After reading the version printed above in *Granny on the Roofrack*, Richard Snedden, an English teacher, remembered hearing this one during the mid–60s. He read it out to his Year 8 class in 1996, and about ten of the group had heard it. It also featured, in one of its variations, in the film *Urban Legend*. In fact, recent research in Britain and America suggests that **The Head** story has taken over from

'The Hook' as the most common adolescent legend. In his *Performance and Practice: Oral Narrative Traditions Among Teenagers in Britain and Ireland* (1997), Michael Wilson writes that possibly up to 100 per cent of twelve- to thirteen-year-olds would know this legend or one of its variants. He even quotes one of his informants having heard a version of the story on an episode of the Australian television soap 'Home and Away', broadcast in the United Kingdom on 9 March 1994, an excellent example of the interaction between popular media and oral transmission.

THE TAPEWORM

Despite having a healthy appetite, a child continued to become thinner and thinner. Fearing that he would waste away, the parents took him to a doctor, who diagnosed that the child had a tapeworm that was eating the food. He said he would treat the child immediately and asked the parents to wait outside.

After a long wait, the parents became concerned. They peered into the surgery to see the doctor dangling a piece of meat on a string in front of the child's open mouth. From the mouth appeared the first few centimetres of a long tapeworm, attracted by the food.

In some versions the mother faints and the story ends there. In others, she screams in horror and frightens the child, who sucks the tapeworm back into its throat and chokes to death.

I remember being terrified and repulsed by this one for years after I first heard it as a kid. The story takes many forms and occurs in all sorts of places to all sorts of people.

It is known in the folklore trade as 'The Bosom Serpent', a quaintly archaic term that indicates the antiquity of the basic story, while also hiding its repulsiveness.

The grotesque nature of this tale does not seem to have affected its long history and diffusion. In fact, the sheer awfulness of the events has probably been the main reason for the story's popularity since at least the sixteenth century. In one form or another, the tale has been told, written, drawn and filmed (in *Alien*, 1979, and its sequels).

The unwelcome internal guest can also frequently be a snake or a frog, as well as a tapeworm. Scholars have researched this one in depth and spent a great deal of time analysing its meaning(s). You can choose from Freudian, medical or cultural interpretations, or just settle for the 'yuk factor'.

An English folklorist collected a version of this tale in 1916.

A woman was said to have swallowed a frog's egg, and it grew inside her. She was taken to hospital but the doctors were unable to operate because the frog was moving around inside her too violently. In agony, the woman begged to be put out of her misery by poisoning, so the doctors consulted the king to see if they could perform a mercy killing. The king refused permission and, in desperation, the doctor put a small piece of cheese on the victim's tongue, luring the frog up from her stomach. Unfortunately, on the way out, the frog choked the woman to death.

More recently, in August 2000, an updated version was circulating through the networks of youthlore. Apparently, a baby born in India was found to have the foetus of another child growing inside it. The baby, and presumably its intestinal traveller, were killed by doctors.

THE SEVERED FINGERS

A young man and woman went to a drive-in movie and, comfortably seated in their Volkswagen 'Beetle', settled down to enjoy the film. In the car next door a group of louts were drinking, swearing and generally hooning about, so the young man asked them to quieten down and refrain from using such bad language in front of a woman.

After the show, the louts got out of their car and approached the young couple. The man and woman quickly wound up the windows and locked the doors, and the man attempted to start the car. Before he could drive away, however, the louts lifted up the back wheels of the Beetle, preventing it from gaining traction (the VW is a rear-wheel-drive car), and one of the men tried to force open the car windows.

In a panic, the young man stepped hard on the accelerator just as the louts, the weight of the car too much for them, dropped the rear wheels back onto the ground. The Beetle screeched off and the couple escaped, but when they arrived home and climbed gratefully out of the car they found two bloody fingers hanging from the rear bumper bar.

There are several versions of **The Severed Fingers** circulating in Australia. Folklorist John Meredith recalls hearing the story during the 1950s, when it supposedly took place at Parramatta Lake, New South Wales. The tale also surfaced in Brisbane and Sydney during the 1960s.

While the details vary, the same story has been told in

Britain since at least the 1960s and it is also known throughout Europe and the United States. This yarn has been traced back to a sixteenth century French legend about a robber whose fingers are lopped off as he tries to grab the bridle of a passing horse. There are also numerous tales about people severing their fingers, or having them severed, in Celtic and other folklores. As with many of the 'contemporary' legends, this one has a considerable history in one form or another.

According to a variation from the Perth *Sunday Times* of 14 November 1993, a Rolls Royce pulled up at some traffic lights and was attacked by a group of inebriated youths. The youths bounced the Rolls up and down by lifting the rear bumper, but the lights changed and the Rolls roared off. When the driver reached his garage and inspected the damage he found a bleeding thumb, caught in the bumper.

You might remember much the same yarn being used in the futuristic film *Mad Max II*, where a yobbo's hand gets painfully similar, but deserved, treatment. That was a long time ago, of course, but since then this tale of just deserts has continued to appal us and enthral us. It is also known in New Zealand in versions that often feature the offending fingers clamped in the car door frame or wrapped in a bike chain hooked to the boot handle, a variation that is also quite common in Australian tellings of the tale.

AN EARWIG ON THE BRAIN

While a woman lay on the beach, an earwig crawled into her ear. She went home, thinking no more about it until a few days later when she experienced a painful earache. The woman consulted a doctor, who examined the ear and found the

earwig deep inside but couldn't get it out. 'You'll have to wait until it comes out the other side,' the doctor told her.

A week or two later, the insect emerged from the other ear, and the woman caught it and returned it to the doctor. 'I'm afraid it's a female,' he informed her after examining the creature. 'It's probably laid its eggs in your head and when they hatch, they'll eat their way through your brain.'

An Earwig on the Brain is quite widely known and people will swear that they know of someone to whom it happened — well, an earwig crawled in their ear, at least. I doubt that it's anatomically possible for an insect to get any further than the ear, and certainly not to the brain. And do earwigs live on the beach? But perhaps we should be just a little bit more careful at the beach on our next holiday.

It's not just earwigs or spiders that get you at the beach, either. On 17 September 1996, British newspaper the *Guardian* reported an item carried in the journal of weird and wonderful phenomena, *The Fortean Times*. According to this story a Swedish backpacker named Magnus Carlstedt had to be taken by ambulance from a hostel at Bondi Beach to have a two-inch long cockroach removed from inside his ear. This just goes to show that the British still see Australia as a foreign place.

This 'modern' legend seems to be anything but. In an intriguing piece of historical investigation, Jan Brunvand discovered that the word 'earwig' is in fact an Old or Middle English term for an 'ear bug', presumably reflecting a thousand-year-old belief that these particular insects are partial to a bit of ear and brain. There is certainly a widespread belief, recorded in America and Britain, that 'earwigs' are so called because of their attraction to that part of the human anatomy.

HORRIBLE
EMBARRASSMENTS

THE DINNER PARTY

When a woman was asked by her business-executive husband to prepare a very important dinner party for some high-flying colleagues and their fussy wives, she panicked. Finally, after much deliberation, she decided what she would serve. The menu would include an entrée of salmon mousse.

Just hours before the guests were due to arrive, she began to prepare the fish for the mousse when the telephone rang and she rushed out to answer it, leaving the fish on the bench. On returning to the kitchen she discovered the cat on the bench, eating the salmon.

'Get down, Mog!' she shouted, and quickly cut off the bit of salmon the cat had chewed.

The evening went off without a hitch and was a great success. But as the last guests departed, the hosts spied their cat lying in the front garden, dead. 'Oh my God,' the woman exclaimed. 'There must have been something wrong with the salmon!'

They quickly rang to warn their former guests who, on hearing the terrible news, went straight to hospital to have their stomachs pumped.

The following morning the next-door neighbour appeared at the back door. Apologising profusely, he explained that he had run over the cat.

'I didn't see him. It was dark, and he was in the middle of our driveway. I could see you had guests and I didn't want to spoil the party. So I put the cat's body in the garden, and I thought I'd break the bad news to you today.'

A version of **The Dinner Party** was published in *The Sydney Morning Herald* in October 1986. The newspaper initially claimed that the incident had taken place, but later withdrew this assertion. The story was also collected in Perth in April 1987, from a twenty-two-year-old male electrical engineer who remembered reading it in a *Post* magazine around 1985.

In Australia, **The Dinner Party** can be traced back to the 1940s. George Blaikie's book *Remember Smith's Weekly* (1966), on the famously irreverent newspaper *Smith's Weekly*, reports that the same yarn was sent to the paper by a reader — an important indication of its oral circulation — and published in December 1944. That story concerned a high-society dinner party in Elizabeth Bay, Sydney, at which the hostess served, in dainty sandwiches, the wartime rarity of pink salmon. In the same week the Melbourne *Age* printed a version of the tale, allegedly from Washington, DC. A couple of weeks later, the *Brisbane Truth* printed a version set in a country town in Queensland. The Sydney *Sun* carried a short story on the same theme and, in January 1945, the Adelaide *Advertiser* and the *Bulletin* printed versions of the story. The Melbourne *Sun-Pictorial* gave a cash prize to a short story on the same theme in March, much to *Smith's* published disgust. 'Anyhow, we had it first,' *Smith's* reckoned. Maybe, but somehow I doubt it.

The Dinner Party is a chestnut that turns up all over the world. Sometimes it involves salmon dishes of one kind or another; sometimes the pet is the family cat, sometimes the family dog. The constants seem to be the flashiness of the dinner party and the unpleasant pumping of stomachs, while the implied undercutting of wealth and pretension seems to appeal to the Australian sense of egalitarianism. The moral, of course, is beware of jumping to hasty conclusions!

A FART IN THE DARK

There was a man who had a penchant for foods that would make him fart. His wife became so sick of his farting that she forbade him to eat any more beans. One day however, he couldn't resist them any longer, so at lunch time at work he ate this whole pile of baked beans.

That evening when he arrived home, his wife told him that she had arranged a surprise for him. Blindfolding him, she sat him down at the table. 'Stay there and I'll be back in a minute,' she ordered.

He waited and waited but she didn't return. Deciding to make the most of the opportunity, he let off a cracker of a fart, and then sighed in relief and satisfaction. Seconds later the man's wife came back and whipped off the blindfold. He was greeted by the sight of all his relatives and friends sitting around the table, collapsing from the smell.

The story of the flatulent male mistakenly assuming, for various reasons, that he is alone has been knocking round the English-speaking world since the early twentieth century. The above version of **A Fart in the Dark** is a contemporary reworking of a classic yarn about acute embarrassment, and was told in the late 1980s in Western

Australia. Paul Smith tells a British version under the title 'The Bean Feast', in his 1983 book *The Book of Nastier Legends*.

Versions of this embarrassing story also circulate in photocopy form. The following variation was doing the rounds of photocopiers in Sydney in 1983 It is related to another piece of fart-lore popular in Australia, and elsewhere, sometimes known as 'The Bean Feast' but titled below **Peas–Peas–Peas** in a text taken from an A4 photocopy.

PEAS-PEAS-PEAS

A knockabout youth married a very refined girl, so he decided to reform his uncouth ways.

He loved to eat peas, but unfortunately they made him fart explosively. Knowing that anything of this nature would be very distasteful to his wife, he went for a whole year without tasting a solitary pea.

But then the craving got too much, his resistance broke, and he went to the local pie cart and ate his fill of pies and peas. Since he lived in an outer suburb, he felt he could get rid of any unpleasant reactions before he reached home. Although he farted all the way home, he was still highly volatile when he reached the house.

His genteel wife met him at the door, threw her arms around his neck and cried 'Oh John, I have the most wonderful surprise for you for your dinner tonight. It's in the dining room now. Let me blindfold you before you go in.'

He submitted to the blindfold and she led him into the dining room and sat him at his usual place at the head of the table. By this time he was desperately fighting off the rumblings that were threatening to erupt and which would surely disrupt his happy home. Then the telephone rang, and after he had promised her that he would not take off the blindfold until she returned, his wife ran to answer it.

This was the husband's big opportunity. Standing up and bending forward slightly, he unleashed a mighty fart which thundered around the room and hung heavily in the air. In a panic to clear the air before his wife returned he groped around the table, fumbling for a napkin, which he frantically swished up and down.

By the time his wife came back into the room the husband had a contented look on his face and was completely at peace with the world.

'Now for your surprise,' she said, as she slipped the blindfold from his eyes. And there it was — twelve dinner guests seated around the table in stunned silence.

How easy it is! A clear warning here — don't take anything for granted and look before you ...

Fascination with farting is widespread in folklore worldwide. The German trickster Till Eulenspiegel is credited with legendary feats of wind-breaking. Heroic farting is also found in *The 1001 Nights* and in the Korean tale of *General Pumpkin*, whose thunderous farts destroy walls and paralyse ravening white tigers. Usually in these older traditions, the flatulent hero is unembarrassed by his explosions, instead revelling in their strength and stink. While this is an interesting point of difference between older and newer tales of this type, it remains true that farting seems to be the domain of males in folklore past and present. Hmm.

Further on the fascinating subject of intestinal fortitude, or lack of it, in *Granny on the Roofrack* I mentioned a new legend I had been told. It concerned a teacher who, in an effort to be healthy and regular, over-indulged on fibre supplements. One morning at breakfast he really loaded up on fibre and by the time he got to work was feeling distinctly unwell in the tummy region. Nevertheless, he went on to take his class. The rumbling in his tummy grew louder and more volcanic by the minute and eventually the pressure became so great that his tummy exploded all over the class. They took him to hospital, but he didn't make it.

While reading a book nicely titled *The Prevalence of Nonsense* by Ashley Montagu and Edward Darling (1967), I came across mention of a similar story. The authors told how, in some parts of the United States, it is believed that when certain foods (exactly *which* foods varied from place to place) are eaten with other foods present in the intestine they react in an explosive manner. As they put it, 'We are not referring to a little gas on the stomach: what is meant is an interior bomb that will blow you up — and out.' They then quoted someone they described as 'the well-known authority Dr Jean Bogert' to the effect that: 'The substances of which food are made up are rather inert chemically, so that there is very little chemical reaction taking place between them and no possibility of their forming explosive mixtures in the stomach'.

Ahh, the relief.

ASHES TO ASHES

A Dutch family had emigrated to Australia, leaving the family farm and their relatives behind. Each year at harvest time the relatives back home would send over a box of apples from the farm, with which the family would make a huge apple pie.

One year the box of apples also contained a small plastic bag of grey powder. Assuming the powder was a special spice for the apples, the mother added the new spice to the pie. It was especially delicious, and the pie was all eaten by the time a letter, which had been delayed, arrived from the Netherlands.

'We're sending you the annual box of apples,' the letter said. 'Hope you enjoy them. But the sad news is that Uncle Herman died last week. And as you loved him so much, we thought we'd send you his ashes.'

This unsettling little tale, collected by Dave Hults in 1987, always seems to involve migration, as well as the unfortunate lack of communication about the nature of the grey powder. Sometimes the mysterious powder is said to be a 'secret ingredient' in a traditional family recipe.

Speculation about what such an unsettling story might mean has included suggestions that it's related to ancestor worship or cannibalism. The 1960s British version, recorded in Rodney Dale's *The Tumour in the Whale* (1978), reverses the geography and has the ashes arriving in England from Australia, and suggests the tale is about family ties sundered through migration. There's also the implied warning of making sure you know what you are eating, a theme that is central in 'contamination legends' (see Chapter 4).

According to Jan Brunvand's discussion of this story in his book *Too Good to Be True: The Colossal Book of Urban Legends* (1999), a 1990 BBC radio program included a letter from a listener whose family had consumed half the ashes of a relative returned from Australia, before receiving the letter telling them the dreadful truth.

BODILY FLUIDS

A man bought an old house of grand proportions. In the wine cellar he discovered a large wooden barrel, full of the finest rum. The family spent the next year or so gradually emptying the barrel, consuming rum at every meal.

Eventually it became difficult to get any more of the liquor out of the barrel, so the family decided to cut it open, to release the last of the flavoursome dregs. To their horror, they found a thoroughly pickled human corpse.

A similar story was told about sailors drinking from the rum cask that carried the body of Lord Nelson home from the Battle of Trafalgar. Many readers will also have heard the tale of the human remains found in the local water-supply during annual maintenance.

An exquisite variation on this theme comes from Western Australian railway-lore.

One hot day in the desert the passengers on the Meekatharra Mail were relieved by the kindness of the guard bringing everyone a drink of ice water. As the day got hotter and the air drier, the passengers continued to quench their thirst with glasses of ice water provided by the guard. But after a few hours, the welcome chilled fluid stopped coming. As the guard passed along the passageway on his duties, a thirsty passenger inquired why the ice water had dried up.

'Sorry,' replied the guard, 'I thought we'd better not drink any more — the body's beginning to show through the ice.'

DREADFUL ACCIDENTS

THE EXPLODING DUNNY

A woman was having difficulty exterminating a particularly stubborn cockroach, so she threw it into the toilet and gave it a good spray of insecticide. Immediately afterwards her husband rushed in, urgently needing to use the loo. Comfortably settled in, he finished the cigarette he was smoking and dropped the butt between his legs into the bowl. There was an immediate explosion as the insecticide and other gaseous elements ignited.

With a badly burned rear and genitals, the man was in agony and in need of urgent medical attention. On arrival at the house, the ambulance men were told the news of the dreadful accident. They all burst out laughing. Bundling the man face-down onto a stretcher they began to carry the victim out, but their laughter became uncontrollable and they dropped the stretcher. The poor patient hit the concrete driveway with a thud. Now the victim had a broken pelvis as well as a blackened backside.

Basically an updated version of a venerable piece of country yokel humour, **The Exploding Dunny** comes in a number of forms. In its bush-yarn form the story is set in the days before septic tanks and sewers, when the traditional dunny was a hole in the ground. As the hole began to fill, the usual practice was to pour kerosene down to disguise the smell and aid decomposition. One day someone mistakenly poured petrol down the hole and the next person to use the dunny dropped his lighted cigarette butt into it. The resulting explosion variously blows up the dunny, its contents and the unfortunate smoker.

In other versions of this modern legend, a man goes to the toilet immediately after it's been cleaned with a high-powered new toilet cleanser. He sits down with the paper, lights up a smoke and throws the butt into the bowl, with the same unhappy results.

This 'hilarious accident' tale is told around Australia and around the world. Like many legends, it sometimes makes it into the mass media. On 31 August 1988, *The Sydney Morning Herald* published an account of the yarn that had appeared in an Israeli newspaper as a true story. The paper later admitted that the story was not true, but by then it had been taken up by other newspapers. Paul Smith's 1983 British-published collection, *The Book of Nasty Legends*, includes a version (broken legs), Jan Brunvand has an English version in his 1986 collection *The Mexican Pet*, and Ron Edwards retells one or two in his *Fred's Crab and other Bush Yarns* (1989), including one collected in 1960 from a digger who reckoned it happened in training camp in 1940 (but no subsequent accident as ambulance-men collapse with laughter).

Old though it is, the exploding dunny continues to divert us. After reading *Granny on the Roofrack*, Annabelle James of Winnellie sent me a clipping from the *Northern Territory News* of 18 September 1997. The article reports that a metalworker from Hong Kong had been taking a lunchtime nap on the factory toilet. It was fairly gloomy in there, so he flicked on his cigarette lighter to check his watch, and went up in flames.

Annabelle, recognising this as a likely urban legend after reading my previous book, pointed out the news story to her husband, telling him that it was remarkably similar to many other such stories. Unimpressed with his wife's new-found knowledge, Mr James, who obviously does not share his wife's taste in books, replied, 'But this one's fair dinkum. It's gone to court'.

The continued popularity of this fable is perhaps due to its moral — even the most mundane domestic places and activities can be dangerous. Smokers, you have been warned.

THE LOADED RABBIT

A rabbit-oh, new to the task of catching bunnies, was not having too much luck. No matter what he did, he couldn't seem to bag a single bunny. The old hands were doing well, so the new bloke decided to ask them for advice. They told him to get himself a rabbit, tie a stick of gelignite to its tail, light the 'gelly' and send the rabbit down the nearest burrow. This would guarantee a big, if messy, haul.

The new bloke thought that this was a fine idea. The only trouble was he couldn't catch a rabbit in the first place, so he decided to buy himself one from the pet store in town. Back in the bush, he removed the rabbit from its cage, tied the gelly to it, lit the fuse and pointed the animal towards the burrows. Off went the rabbit, but, having been born in captivity, it didn't know what to do in the wild. The rabbit circled round and round and ran back towards the bloke, fuse spluttering. It finally scurried underneath his expensive new ute, blowing the whole thing to buggery.

This is really a modernised old bush yarn which also has a lengthy history as an international tale, being known in Europe as far back as the Middle Ages, and even in India. Like many other such widely distributed stories, it has been traced to the Bible.

In the updated stories, it is usually a couple of blokes, often out hunting, who tie the gelignite to the rabbit out of cruelty. The rabbit, which is a wild one rather than tame, is terrified and does the same thing as the traditional bunny, running under the blokes' $50,000 four-wheel drive where, of course, it explodes.

In these contemporary versions the cruelty of the men (rather than the need to earn a living, as in the bush yarn) and the value of the automobile are the important elements, while the image of the exploded rabbit provides a grisly dimension that is characteristic of urban legends.

Other modern versions of this are reported widely in North America, they often pop up in the press — there is even an exploding fish variation. As far as the Australian renditions, both old and new, are concerned, it doesn't seem to be stretching credibility too far to suggest that Henry Lawson knew the yarn and used it in his well-known short story 'The Loaded Dog', as did Jack London, who used the same situation a few years later in his 1902 story 'Moon-Face'. In Queensland they seem to prefer exploding pigs that write off the ute in exactly the same way.

THE HEADLESS BIKIE

As a truckload of corrugated iron (or some other form of metal sheeting) was being driven along the highway, a motorcycle rider drew alongside in the act of overtaking.

At that moment, one of the sheets blew off the truck and decapitated the bikie.

But the headless bikie didn't fall over. His hands gripped the accelerator and he continued to overtake the truck. The incredulous truck driver noticed the headless bikie flying by and the shock caused him to have a heart attack. As he lost control, the truck ploughed into a line of people waiting for a bus.

The Headless Bikie is another popular highway horror. Sometimes the story has the truck crashing without injuring or killing anyone else, but it is still a grisly and frequently heard tale. The story has been around in Australia since at least the 1950s and it is well known in Britain. It is still widespread in this country — it was related on Perth radio in August 1987, and undoubtedly in many other places and on many occasions before and since.

[HAIRY STORIES]

REDBACKS IN THE DREADLOCKS

A young man with a mass of dreadlocks went to the hairdresser for a trim. As soon as the female hairdresser touched his head, the young man yelled in pain. Alarmed, she pulled away. When she tried again the man yelled even louder. He told the hairdresser not to worry and left the shop.

On the following day the police called into the shop to tell the hairdresser that the young man was dead. When the woman touched his head she had disturbed a horde of redback spiders nesting in the dreadlocks and they had poisoned him to death.

The age-old fear of humans being infested with insects is updated in this recent legend, which should be compared with those concerning earwigs in the brain — see **The Bouffant Hairdo** and **An Earwig on the Brain**.

The story here is probably more than just a little prejudice against those who are 'different'. This originally Rastafarian hairstyle has been adopted in recent years by some youth sectors and many people feel that dreadlocks are too long and unkempt to be 'hygienic'. This complaint was also directed at 'long-haired hippies' in the 1960s, about whom the same tale was told. The vengeful tale of the nesting spiders no doubt appeals to those who view long hair with dread.

Redbacks in the Dreadlocks is similar to **The Bali Spiders** (Chapter 5), which also deals with insect infestation, but it is more closely related to another oldie but a goodie from the 1950s and 1960s: **The Bouffant Hairdo**.

THE BOUFFANT HAIRDO

A young woman went to the hair salon and had her hair put up into one of the elaborate bouffant hairstyles that were popular in the late 1950s and 1960s. These were so delicate that they weren't washed but held in place with tins of Gossamer hair lacquer. The style couldn't be messed with and was held by continual spraying.

One morning the girl was found dead. During the night earwigs, which were nesting in the bouffant hairdo, had crawled out into her ear and eaten their way through her brain.

In some versions of the story it is cockroaches rather than earwigs that do the eating, but the end result is the same. Now that bouffants are no longer popular, this tale isn't often heard, although it was reported as common in Britain in Rodney Dale's 1978 collection, *The Tumour in the Whale*. The story has a modern offspring in **Redbacks in the Dreadlocks**, however, and it may also be told without the obsolete hairdo themes. This is often a simple moral tale involving a young girl who kept her hair in a beehive hairstyle for nearly six months without washing or shampooing it. When she finally took her hair down it was found that spiders had laid eggs in her hair and their young had started to feed on her scalp. The girl went mad and had to be put into an asylum.

This only slightly less horrifying version was collected in September 1985, from a young woman who had been told the tale by her mother when she was a child during the 1970s. It shows how contemporary legends are almost infinitely flexible, constructed as it is from elements of **The Bouffant Hairdo** and **Redbacks in the Dreadlocks**. Instead of dying, this poor soul just ended up in the madhouse. While we might think that this story is probably no older than the 1950s, the heyday of the beehive hairstyle, industrious scholars have unearthed medieval precedents of the tale in which a woman who spends too long doing her hair is always late for mass. Eventually the devil possesses her in the form of a spider that comes to live in her hair.

Spiders also appear in folk tradition in various guises. Sometimes they are unlucky, as when a large one is seen on someone's clothing, said to be a sign of imminent death. On the other hand, a small spider is a 'money spider' and is said to be a sign of imminent wealth. Spiders or their webs are used in folk medicine as cures for ague, various forms of bleeding and whooping cough. They are also thought to bring good luck and to deliberately kill one is to bring ill fortune. On this belief, the gentleman with the dreadlocks should be a very fortunate and wealthy man.

Hair is likewise the subject of considerable folk belief. It was thought wise to dispose of cut hair otherwise bad luck would be likely to befall you. This was probably related to the belief that a lock of someone's hair could be used in black magic attacks on an individual. Hair also features strongly in techniques for divining the future, especially in relation to affairs of the heart.

Hair also has a place in other parts of the human anatomy, though.

THE FATAL HAIRBALL

HAIRBALL KILLS GIRL
A British teenager died from eating her own hair. Rachel Haigh, a trainee hairdresser, had chewed her own hair for years, caused a knotted mass of hair the size of a rugby ball to build up inside her.

This item appeared in the *West Australian* of 21 August 1999 and was also published in many other newspapers. The day before the original Associated Press story had appeared on the Urban Legends Reference webpage maintained by the San Fernando Valley Folklore Society. The poster, a 'Sharon

"Hair today, gone tomorrow" Weintraub', wondered if this was 'An urban legend come true?'

Sharon was right to wonder. She sent the full text of the AP story which screamed 'urban legend'. The story told of a seventeen-year-old girl who had died after having a massive hairball removed from her stomach. The hairball was a result of the girl's habit of chewing her hair. Medical experts confirmed that the hair was the girl's own, and professed amazement at the size and thickness of the ball. Her mother was quoted to the effect that while her daughter had chewed her hair when younger, she thought that she had grown out of the habit. When the doctors showed the mother a photograph of the removed hairball she exclaimed that it resembled a dead rat.

This brought a response from the website moderator querying why a death that occurred more than eight months earlier was suddenly being reported as a news story.

A good question, although the inquest findings may have explained the delay. As well as this fact, the oddity of the circumstances, the apparently insensitive comments of the mother about the hairball looking like a dead rat and the obvious cautionary element to the tale are all classic hallmarks of the urban legend, which according to Jan Brunvand's collection of legends in *The Mexican Pet* has been doing the rounds since the mid-1980s.

In 1994, urban legend newsgroup alt.folklore.urban posted a query about hairball death stories. They had generally been regarded as false, until an Ian A. York from Harvard University posted a suggested modification of this entry. He provided five medical journal references showing that hairball deaths, while unusual, did occur. One of these references was from the *Australian and New Zealand Journal of Surgery* 64 (4), 1994. An article by A. Mekesic and E. Farmer saying that trichobezoars (the medical term for hairballs) are rare but 'most commonly occur in young females'. Other references — decidedly unpleasant — from European and American medical journals told much the same story, including one that had a snappy folkloric name for the problem, 'The Rapunzel Syndrome'.

On the basis of this medical evidence, York suggested that the classification of all hairball stories should be modified from 'False' to 'True', with the line saying something like: 'People who chew their hair excessively can develop honkin' great gastrointestinal hairballs, which can be fatal.'

So, are they urban legends or not? The answer is, almost always. Most are false, but one or two will turn out to be true, regardless of how far fetched they might sound. The above story provides a good example of the often murky line between true and false that characterises some urban legends. While most of the friend-of-a-friend stories that are told are false, there are now enough documented cases of 'real' urban legends happening to show that fact and fantasy do sometimes intersect, though it doesn't happen very often. Because someone was unfortunate enough to die from the Rapunzel Syndrome somewhere, or because someone's backside was once burned by an exploding dunny, doesn't mean that every telling of the tale is true. More than likely, it will be an urban legend.

This may be a case of a 'true' urban myth doing some good. Basically, it's not a great idea to chew your hair. Another example of a 'true' urban myth having a positive outcome, though with some ongoing side effects, is the **Redemption by Postcard** story (Chapter 7).

4

TAKING CARE OF BUSINESS

THE WORLD OF BUSINESS and commerce has generated many legends characteristic of the modern era of corporatisation and, increasingly, of globalisation. Almost all urban legends that circulate in Australia are told, in one version or another, in many other parts of the world. With the growth of access to the Internet in the form of the World Wide Web and e-mail, rumours about products and the companies that make them have become increasingly common.

This chapter includes a selection of the many product legends that have been, and continue to be circulated about prominent corporations and household brands. Some of these are 'contamination legends' that trade on what seem to be our considerable fear of adulteration or other contamination of foodstuff — fast foods in particular.

Business and commerce is the natural location for misinformation about money. These can be relatively minor hoaxes, such as the belief that if you peel the wrappers off a pack of Marlboro cigarettes and send in the serial number to Marlboro HQ, you might win a good deal of money. The same story used to circulate about Wrigley's stick chewing gum wrappers in the 1950s and 60s.

The other end of this spectrum is where we find the deliberate attempts to separate us from our hard-earned money. A number of 'get-rich-quick' scams and takes are included here because they trade on our unguarded concerns, and operate in similar ways to urban legends. Hopefully readers will be forewarned about some of the many such cons that purvey misinformation and impossible promises. Although the jury is still out on **The Millennium Bug**, the hype and hysteria that surrounded this alarm is also included.

A few oldies but goodies in the realm of business humour are still doing the rounds. Many business legends and rumours relate to particular brand names. Invariably, these are the high profile and better-known products and companies. For legal reasons, these business cannot be named — but we all know who they are. The final section gives people in business some tips on managing the damage that can be and has been the consequence of urban legends and rumours.

PRODUCT CONTAMINATIONS

SEVERAL GROSS ASSORTED CONTAMINATION RUMOURS

The basic contamination legends are perfectly believable and have been documented as actually occurring. They involve delightful experiences such as finding a foreign object (fingernail, glass, dead insect, etc) in your soft drink or takeaway food.

In April 1997, Marie Henriques bit into a Topic chocolate bar she had purchased at a kiosk in central London. After getting about three-quarters of the way through, she realised that instead of biting on nice chewy hazelnuts, she was in fact relishing the crushed skull, teeth and backbone of a mouse. Poor Marie couldn't face the thought of cooking anything for a long time, it was claimed in *The Times* of December 19 1998.

The makers of Topic, Mars UK (of the famous bars) were taken to court by the Westminster City Council. The red stains found on Marie's teeth, at first thought to be rodent blood, were found on examination by the Natural History Museum to more likely be dye used in rat baits popular in Turkey, the country from which the hazelnuts in the bar were supplied. After considerable scientific investigation and legal proceedings, it was decided that although the hazelnut factory in Turkey was 'technically sophisticated' it was most likely that the mouse got in the Topic bar over there, and certainly not in England. However, Mars was unable to reclaim its legal costs and a spokesperson was quoted as saying: 'Over the past forty years millions of Topic bars have been enjoyed without any comparable incident. This is a measure of the strict quality procedures which we demand'.

So, it really has happened, in England at least.

BRAIN TUMOURS

One British-produced energy drink is rumoured to contain a chemical that causes brain tumours. It is claimed that the United States government has banned it because they gave a similar substance to their troops during the Vietnam War, and most of these soldiers have since developed brain tumours. The rumour goes on. The reason that the drink is not banned in Australia is because this country is a British colony, so we are unable to ban British products.

This legend was circulating in 2000 among adolescent consumers of an energy drink. The fear of additives causing cancer or other chronic illnesses is to the fore, and has been a feature of other contamination legends, such as those about artificial sweeteners. There is also more than a touch of the colonial cringe in this story, with the inaccurate claim that Australia is unable to restrict British products.

[AND MUCH WORSE]

HOLD THE MAYO

One particularly revolting variation on the product contamination theme is **Hold the Mayo**. In this story the kitchen hand at a well-known hamburger outlet ejaculates into the mayonnaise.

By late 1994, this story had developed an additional garnish, according to the Internet.

A friend of a friend went for a burger at the local takeaway. As he chomped into the salad-filled bun, he thought that it was rather chewy. Being in a hurry though, he didn't investigate. When he got near the end of the burger, he eventually dissected it and discovered a green condom hidden amongst the lettuce leaves.

Fortunately, this story spared us the detail of whether or not the condom was used. Given the earlier versions of this one though, it's only a matter of time.

There are many variations on the contaminated fast-food theme, including the following legend.

CONCENTRATED ORANGE JUICE

'One of the guys at (a well-known fast-food outlet) was working late, on the clean-up shift, and he urinated into the orange juice but no-one noticed it because the OJ was so concentrated. So nobody really knew about it until he told everyone afterwards! That was about three years ago — one of the staff members who was there when it happened told me the story.'

Other contamination legends include the dead, but well-preserved, snake in the bottle of whisky; the finger in the meat pie; the mouse's head in the fruit and nut chocolate bar; maggots in the hot dog; the rat in the pizza; and, appropriately for Australia, the flies in the pies. While many of these stories simply lead the listener into wallowing in the awfulness of the experience, some versions have the unfortunate eater of fried rat or other contaminant dying of the effects. More often, however, it is simply sickness of one kind or another that is the alleged outcome of these dubious meals, but these resulting illnesses can be pretty severe.

The legends mentioned so far in this chapter have all been around for many years. But urban legends are always being reworked, usually to make them even worse than they were before. This is certainly true of contamination legends, as the following example illustrates.

HOLD EVERYTHING!

It is Friday evening in any Australian suburb. A few friends are sitting around the table having a drink and a laugh. Into the conversation comes a story about a friend of a friend who had gone for a meal at a local restaurant 'recently'.

The woman ordered a well-done steak at a popular steakhouse. When the meal arrived, it was so rare that she sent it back for further cooking. The steak returned cooked to her satisfaction but as it was very large she was unable to finish it and requested a 'doggy bag' for the remainder of the meal.

By the time she reached home she was not feeling very well and became suspicious that there was something wrong with the steak. The next day she sent it 'for analysis'. When the results came back, they said that the steak was covered with the semen of four men.

The woman is suing the restaurant concerned and it will soon be in all the newspapers.

Collected in Perth in early 2000, this is a widespread and long-standing 'urban legend'. Jane, a caller to a JJJ radio talkback show on 22 May 1998, recounted this one being told in Brisbane at that time. In the Brissie versions the tests show that the meat is contaminated with either herpes or hepatitis. The local restaurant where it is alleged to have occurred was suffering a severe loss of custom as a result, and there was also the suggestion of legal proceedings. Another caller rang in to say that much the same yarn was spinning around Adelaide and Sydney. The talkback show host recalled hearing much the same whopper about five years earlier.

This is one example of the way in which urban legends and rumours can damage businesses. Similar unpleasant stories of deliberate food adulteration circulate about other food chains and products, as well as restaurants with an Asian connection.

American variations of this one were circulating in the 1980s and 1990s, targeting a variety of fast food chains. These legends claimed that the semen carried not herpes or hepatitis, but the AIDS virus. In early 1990 one pizza chain sought the help of urban legend guru Jan Brunvand. He wrote a piece for their company newsletter analysing such rumours and providing employees with advice on how to handle them. In his *Too Good to Be True: The Colossal Book of Urban Legends* (1999), Brunvand concedes that his efforts did not help much as the legend broke out again in 1993. In that outbreak, the legend included the detail that the masturbator actually reveals his actions to the luckless people who have consumed the pizza, either in person or by telephone.

[OTHER BUSINESS PROBLEMS]

THE DEATH CAR

A used-car dealer had an expensive late-model car for sale at a ridiculously low price — a couple of hundred dollars — but no matter how cheap, no-one would buy the car. It seemed that someone had committed suicide in the back seat and, despite

being cleaned and disinfected, the smell of death just wouldn't go away. As soon as potential buyers got close enough to smell it, they didn't want the car.

This cheery little tale persists, even though it seems somewhat unrealistic. In some versions of the story the car has to be burned or otherwise disposed of. In others, the expensive vehicle is said to be rusting away on a local used-car lot.

The Death Car has been told in America since the late 1930s and has been tracked back to the early 1950s in Britain. Known in Russia and Poland, it has been around in Australia since at least the 1960s and is sometimes told in combination with certain aspects of **The Divorcee's Revenge** (Chapter 2).

TELSTRA AND OPTUS 90#

In 1998, a rumour began circulating that it was possible for someone to make calls on your mobile phone account by dialling 90# then your mobile phone number. Telstra was bombarded with thousands of calls from worried mobile customers, many of whom heard about this through the Internet, especially by e-mail. In November 1998, Telstra issued a press release stating: 'Dialling 90# will absolutely NOT allow a third party to make calls on your account, or otherwise interfere with your mobile service'. As well, the engineers at Cable & Wireless Optus found that it was not possible to do this. Despite these and other credible refutations, the belief is still in circulation at the time of writing, mid–2001.

Like many rumours and urban legends, this one seems to have its origins in at least a grain of truth. Apparently it was possible in the early 1990s for some American PABX phone systems to be used by an outside caller if someone inside the company dialled the number for them. That scam ended and it never applied to mobile phones, only to those connected to some types of PABXs.

Despite these refutations, the legend lives. So, it seems, does 'old nick'.

[HEARSAY]

THE GREAT BARCODE BEAST AND OTHER NUMBERS

Fundamentalist Christian groups of various persuasions seem to be the originators and disseminators of many of the Satanist rumours and legend scares. Such groups habitually circulate extreme, if not bizarre, interpretations of the Scriptures and current affairs orally and in print form. A persistent example involves the 'mark of the great beast' — 666 — that has been given an update through the introduction of barcode technology.

One such group distributed a leaflet that appeared in some Perth mailboxes in late 1996, claiming that barcodes contain the number 666. Quoting slabs of Revelation, which refers to the number of the beast as 666, the flyer claimed that 'Satan will give power to the Antichrist to control the whole world with the use of the computerised system 666' (barcode or Microchip). Elsewhere we read: 'Coding of 666 has already been concealed on all consumer goods. Recently in America, it is not only being stamped on animals, but as well being encouraged for human hand or on the forehead'. The document also featured a technological updating of the barcode mark, namely the implantable bio-chip, that would have the same sinister effect. A slightly altered version of this document was circulating in Sydney during August 1998. Both versions may derive from an article published in the magazine *Nexus*, vol. 2, June–July 1994.

It is difficult to discern from these documents just why the Antichrist is going to all this trouble. Clearly it is not for our betterment, and involves, unsurprisingly, the Day of Judgement.

Such apparently irrational beliefs are hardly restricted to Christian cultures, and can have a serious impact upon those who take them seriously. It was reported in *The Weekend Australian* of 21–22 December 1996, that the authorities in charge of public utilities in the San Gabriel Valley, east of Los Angeles, announced that they were going to change the 818 area code to 626. The large Chinese population in the area were horrified at the change as in southern Chinese, Taiwanese and Hong Kong cultures, there is a powerful numerological tradition that the number 8 is lucky. Thus, the 818 area code was very lucky, and was one of the main reasons why many Chinese families had moved to the area in the first place. Matters were made even worse by the fact that the new area code, 626, added up to 14, and the number 4 is associated with death in this belief tradition, because of the similarity between the pronunciation of the numbers and the Mandarin and Cantonese words for 'luck' and 'death'.

Similar difficulties were reported in *The Weekend Australian* of 16–17 August 1997, by Sydney real estate agents. Apparently, the increasing number of migrants with a Chinese background was beginning to influence the street-numbering policies of local councils. It has long been common practice (though not universal) for the number 13 to be excised from hotel floor and room numbers, but now property developers are constructing multistorey apartment blocks without the Chinese equivalent of '4'. One development in Sydney's Chinatown, for instance, even dispensed with levels 14, 24, 34 and 40. Another development has aspired to an apparently admirable multiculturalism and left out all these levels *and* the thirteenth level. But whether this ploy has been successful is doubtful, as according to Chinese beliefs, the number 13 is considered lucky.

GOING BY THE NUMBERS

Back in the 1980s, there was, as now, a heightened concern about food additives and the possible health effects of these, especially on growing children. Many parents were given an A4 sheet listing food additive codes prepared by, or on behalf of, the United Nations, to check what had been added to the foods we were giving to our children. My wife and I continually referred to this list, and it was an important part of our domestic routine.

The sheet of paper consisted of a list of code numbers, usually followed by a selection of the types of food to which they were likely to be added. These were also arranged in accordance with the level of danger each additive threatened — cancer, ADD, diarrhoea and other delights. When we went shopping we carefully scrutinised bottles, tins and packets in the supermarket to make sure they did not contain any of the nasties on our list. The nastiest one of all was number 330 which according to our list, was guaranteed to virtually kill you the moment you ingested it. We were especially vigilant about scanning labels for 330 and avoided it whenever we came across it, which was worryingly often.

Eventually the sheet disappeared into that place where useful but odd scraps of paper go, and we congratulated ourselves on some good parenting. The kids had lived, thrived and grown up. Mission accomplished. Well, yes and no.

On 8 April 1998, an article by dietitian Glen Cardwell appeared in the *West Australian* newspaper. Cardwell was writing about a list of food additives that had been prepared in 1974, allegedly under the auspices of a Paris hospital. It listed 139 food additives with one in particular, code number 330, being the most dangerous carcinogen of all. The list spread rapidly through France and was picked up by the media, eventually causing so much concern that the French Minister of Agriculture was forced to make a statement in July 1976 to allay fears about code number 330.

What was it?

Citric acid. The dreadful sounding code number 330 was nothing more than a substance that occurs naturally in many fruits and is widely used as a preservative in jams, toppings, cordials, confectionery, dessert products and even in pickles. Usually the amounts added to food are much less than would be consumed by eating fruit. Cardwell quoted a number of authorities on the harmlessness of the dreaded 330, citric acid, including Arnold Bender, Professor of Nutrition and Dietetics at the University of London, on the benign nature and widespread use of citric acid.

Oops, we were well and truly taken in. For a while I thought I might even have to surrender my urban legendist badge. More worryingly, by religiously following an unverified piece of paper we might have been depriving our children of necessary vitamins. Guilt, guilt. Fortunately they ate lots of citrus fruit and don't appear to have suffered any ill-effects. What it goes to show, of course, is how easily we can all be taken in by false information.

This contamination hoax operated in the classic manner of the urban legend. It traded on some of our deepest concerns. It was distributed through personal contacts and a well-meaning community group, and it appeared at least to have the sanction of a credible authority. It gave us, and the thousands, perhaps millions of others throughout the world, the unfounded belief that we could do something practical for the health of our children. In this case we were all 'myth-taken'.

[FUNNY BUSINESS]

THE DRUG TRAFFICKER'S TAX DEDUCTION

In an unusual case, a convicted drug trafficker was entitled to a tax deduction for $220,000 which had been buried in his backyard and subsequently stolen during a drug deal.

The court found that the stolen amount was a loss directly connected with the carrying on of his business.

This brief item appeared in a newsletter for accountants and their clients in September 2000. It was printed without any comment of the GST, FBT or any of the other things Canberra likes to foist upon us. This story provides an ideal opportunity for some acid urban legend testing.

Firstly, no source for the information is given. Secondly, neither the drug trafficker or the court where this supposedly took place is named. And lastly, no dates are provided. Such vagueness, coupled with the gobsmacking nature of the situation, screams 'urban legend'.

And, can you really get a tax deduction for stolen money? Check with your accountant. Maybe you can claim your GST.

PISS OFF, REG!

An ambitious businessman was lunching with a potential client in a classy Brisbane restaurant. Anxious to impress the client in order to win his business, the businessman gave a grandiose description of his abilities and the results he could obtain. Just then he noticed that Reg Ansett had entered the restaurant and joined a group of high-flying financiers at a nearby table.

This was too good an opportunity to miss. The businessman excused himself and, although not acquainted with Reg, approached his table and asked to speak with him. Reg granted him an audience, and the businessman said, 'Look Reg, you don't know me from a bar of soap, but would you mind giving a fellow businessman a leg up? All you have to do is say "Hello, very pleased to meet you again" as I go out with my client. Would you do that for me?'

Reg, in a relaxed mood after a lunchtime wine, generously agreed. The businessman thanked him profusely, embarrassingly even, then returned to his table and the waiting client. They finished their drinks, the businessman paid the bill and walked towards the door with his client. Sure enough, as they passed, Reg Ansett kept his word and hailed the man like a long-lost friend.

The businessman looked down. 'Piss off, Reg, can't you see I'm busy with an important client?'

This well-travelled story usually features a prominent business figure. This particular version was often heard in Australia in the 1980s and since. Of course, it really happened in Sydney, Adelaide, Hobart, Darwin ... I haven't heard this one again lately, but it's too good not to still be in circulation in the business community, and perhaps even further afield.

THE LITTLE RED HEN: AN UPDATE

Once upon a time there was a Little Red Hen who scratched about in the farmyard and uncovered some grains of wheat. She called her neighbours and said, 'If we work together and plant this wheat we will have some fine bread to eat. Who will help me plant it?'

'Not I,' said the duck.

'Not I,' said the goose.

'Not I,' said the cow.

'Not I,' said the pig.

'Then I will,' said the Little Red Hen. And she did.

The wheat grew tall and ripened into golden grain. 'Who will help me reap the wheat?' asked the Little Red Hen.

'Not I,' said the duck.

'Out of my classification,' said the pig.

'I'd lose my unemployment insurance,' said the goose.

'Then I will,' said the Little Red Hen. And she did.

Then it came time to bake the bread.

'That's overtime for me,' said the cow.

'I'm a drop-out and never learnt how,' said the duck.

'I'd lose my welfare benefits,' said the goose.

'Then I will,' said the Little Red Hen. And she did.

She baked five loaves of fine bread and held them up for her neighbours to see.

'I want some,' said the cow.

'I want some,' said the duck.

'I want some,' said the pig.

'I demand my share,' said the goose.

'No,' said the Little Red Hen. 'I can rest for a while and eat the five loaves myself.'

'Excess profit,' cried the cow.

'Capitalistic leech!' screamed the duck.

'Company fink,' grunted the pig.

'Equal rights!' yelled the goose.

And they hurriedly painted picket signs and marched around the Little Red Hen, singing 'We Shall Overcome'. And they did.

For when the farmer came to investigate the commotion, he said 'You must not be greedy, Little Red Hen. Look at the oppressed cow. Look at the disadvantaged duck. Look at the underprivileged pig. Look at the less-fortunate goose. You are guilty of making second-class citizens of them.'

'But I earnt the bread,' said the Little Red Hen.

'Exactly,' said the farmer. 'This is the wonderful free-enterprise system; anybody in the farmyard can earn as much as he wants. You should be happy to have this freedom. In other barnyards you would have to give all five loaves to the farmer. Here you give four to your suffering neighbours and keep one for yourself.'

And they all lived happily ever after, including the Little Red Hen, who smiled and clucked, 'I am grateful.' But her neighbours wondered why she never baked any more bread.

This satirical rewrite of a favourite children's story pillories the failure of the system and those caught in it to recognise and reward entrepreneurial activity and application. Although not strictly an urban legend, as it circulates in photocopy form rather than orally, it is very similar to many legends — both in structure and in its fable-like quality.

An echo of Orwell's *Animal Farm*, **The Little Red Hen: An Update** was popular in Australian workplaces throughout the 1980s, in typed, printed and photocopied versions. Sometimes said to have been written in America in 1975, versions of it have been traced back to at least the early 1970s.

TUPPERWARE TOPS

A young boy imprisoned the family cat in a Tupperware container. Fortunately, his mother discovered the cat just in time and released it. To make sure that if this happened again, the cat wouldn't suffocate, the boy's mother went around the house punching holes in the lids of all her airtight Tupperware containers.

This story came to me by telephone in June 2000, from a friend who heard it from a friend, who heard it from his neighbour. When the friend of a friend phoned his wife, holidaying in the USA at this time, and herself a Tupperware seller, she laughed her head off. Apparently this was an old yarn known to everyone who sold Tupperware.

This story is what folklorists refer to as a noodle or numskull story. These stories involve individuals doing absurd things. Numskulls and noodles are found throughout the world's folklores and Australia has its very own version in the character of 'The Drongo'.

Named after a racehorse that was unable to win a race, the Drongo is a prize fool who takes everything said to him quite literally. When the boss asked him to hang a gate he hung it by a noose from the nearest tree. When the boss asked him to find a pumpkin in the vegetable patch 'the size of your head', he tried his hat on all the pumpkins in the garden. And there's more, but the Drongo is more of a rural than an urban legend, so we'll leave him with the pumpkins.

[SCAMS, CONS AND TAKES]

THE WIZARDS OF WEALTH

There are now many magazines and other publications devoted to 'money making' or 'business opportunities'. While most of these publications are perfectly respectable professional and trade journals, there are some that appear to be nothing more than vehicles for all kinds of weird and wonderful 'get-rich-quick' schemes. These range from 'multi-level marketing' (basically pyramid selling, outlawed in many countries), to 'magic words' (read 'magic spells'); all promising untold riches overnight, or at least next week. Some of these advertisements use methods such as the 'magic words' mentioned above, or describe their product, approach or 'secret' as 'the goose that laid the golden egg'. Others attempt to 'sell the sizzle rather than the sausage' by concocting fantasies that would do a quest-game computer programmer proud and which are structured very much like folk and fairy tales.

Billing himself as 'the greatest business genius of this century', a self-described tycoon offered his secrets in *Australian Business and Money Making Opportunities*, (Nov–Jan 1996–97, p. 55).

He wrote that while deep in debt many years ago, he had stumbled across a dusty old book concealed in the cottage of a rich and powerful man. In the book he discovered the 'amazing formula' of the super rich. He began to use this incredibly simple formula and in six months became a millionaire. Readers were then asked if they would like to know these secrets. Later in the advertisement, the mysterious book is likened to Aladdin's magic lamp. Other get-rich-quick come-ons are similar, often referring to 'magic words' or the 'Midas touch' that will bring wealth.

The same magical methods of obtaining overnight wealth are also found on the Internet. There you will find the 'secrets of success', and other fairy tale formulas offered for sale as in the example that follows, titled **Watch Out for Jennifer Urich**.

Almost all the text in the longer advertisements follows the same narrative pattern, and appears to have been either written by the same person(s) or all derived from a common source, as is often the case with urban legends. Usually the writer (the adverts are always written in the first person) was impoverished and struggling in his (less frequently, her) former life or occupation. Often he has had a sudden, sometimes miraculous enlightenment that provided him with 'the secret of success/wealth/power...' A common variation on this motif is the finding of a document or some other source that contains the secret knowledge required to become rich. This is like finding a map with 'X marks the spot', inherent in lost treasure legends. Then he becomes fabulously rich with ridiculous ease, in an absurdly short period of time. Although he no longer needs to make more money he wants to share the secret of his success with the world. Usually he would be happy to give the secret away for nothing, but he knows that people do not value something that they get for free. Therefore he is forced to charge a fee, though it is insanely low in relation to the value of what the payer will receive. Lastly, the buyer is promised instant, easy success as long as the rules are followed. He too will be able to indulge in the affluent and easy lifestyle of the money magician.

While such fables are not strictly urban legends, they are structured in similar ways and operate in much the same fashion by trading on our emotions. While urban legends press our hidden fear buttons, this sort of scam stabs at the rather common desire to be 'financially independent', the postmodern euphemism for 'filthy rich'. Stick to good old-fashioned thrift and watch out for Jennifer Urich.

WATCH OUT FOR JENNIFER URICH

Over the last few years, as the Internet has expanded into a global business machine, so the get-rich-quick schemes have begun to appear there. The e-mail system is a boon for those using mail order to purvey their money-spinning schemes. Virtually at the touch of a button it is possible to 'spam' — that is, electronically junk mail — hundreds, if not thousands of e-mail addresses. One of these garbled e-mail offers arrived unheralded and unsolicited on my e-mail in August 1997. It came through a network of scholars interested in ballad studies, a topic guaranteed not to make money. Nevertheless, someone calling himself/herself 'Jennifer Urich' ('you rich', get it?) filled the message box of every person on this particular network with an eight paged document headed 'Could you use some extra money?' It used many of the techniques mentioned above and it was clearly related to the kind of 'pyramid selling' outlawed in many countries. It included such refinements as 'Do you have any idea what 11,600 $5 bills ($58,000) look like piled up on a kitchen table? IT'S AWESOME!'

It probably is. I wouldn't know. But it couldn't be as awesome as the garbage peddled by the Jennifer Urichs of the world, whether real or virtual. While the global chaos of the net does not yet allow authorities to stamp out this sort of scam, in Australia at least, we are having a go.

On April Fool's Day 1999, the Australian Securities and Investments Commission (ASIC) established a fake website promising investors ridiculous profits. By 1 May, when the official hoax was revealed, the site had attracted hundreds of customers willing to invest millions in nothing more than an unsubstantiated promise. The investors received an e-mail from ASIC telling them how gullible they had been, and providing them with advice on sensible investment strategies. Let's hope they took it.

THE MILLENNIUM BUG

The recent millennial moment provided a focus for the expression of uncertainty and catastrophe. The end of the world, 'Armageddon' and other such fears are closely allied with the Christian calendar and the wilder reaches of biblical belief. Though many are sceptical about such possibilities, being part of a culture where they are articulated and related to the major nominal form of religious observance, means that they are impossible to avoid totally. Helped along with generous doses of media exposure and movies of global disaster, such as *Asteroid*, and the recent trend for plague scares, there is no escape for any of us.

Was it really surprising, then, that in the gee whizz technological society something called the 'millennium bug' was suddenly spawned? This case of global doomsaying had all the marks of the perfect twentieth-century delusion. It was based on the technological premise that early computer codes used two digits to represent the year — '68' rather than 1968 for example — but it was thought that by 2000 any machines using these codes would have been long obsolete. Therefore, the doomsayers claimed, when the unknown number of machines ticked over their codes at midnight on 31 December 1999, the machines that were not 'compliant' would fail to recognise the final two digits of 2000 and either shut down or react unpredictably. Once this occurred, almost anything might happen, ranging from the minor irritation of your digital timer failing, to the more serious speculations such as aircraft falling from the skies, national power grids shutting down, dams bursting and so on.

This possible problem was first heralded in the late 1970s among the Information Technology (IT) community. It was ignored until 1993, when a number of flamboyant Y2K entrepreneurs began to beat the drums of doom. Books, videos, websites and conferences predicting the worst proliferated, and most countries produced at least one major prophet warning of the dire consequences of Y2K. By 1996, the IT press and eventually the mainstream media were full of Y2K mania. The BBC broadcast a dramatised documentary titled 'The Millennium Time Bomb' in 1998, portraying the devastation of health, emergency and communications facilities, civil unrest and general chaos. Stories and articles on Y2K were increasingly carried in mainstream media, and books advising how to survive the millennium began to appear in increasing numbers. Fringe groups and religious cults began stockpiling food, water and ammunition for the expected apocalypse. Arnold Schwarzenegger saved us, again, from universal extermination and the Great Beast, in the Hollywood movie *End of Days*.

The possibility, no matter how remote, that terrible things would occur was the second element of the belief package that the Y2K industry depended on to support itself. As the alleged outcomes were of such potential concern, no responsible business or government could afford to ignore Y2K, so billions of dollars were spent on testing, and replacement to ensure compliance. Voices of reason soon faded from the debate, such as it was. One of the earliest messengers of a possible problem was Dr Ross Anderson of Cambridge University Computer Laboratory, quoted in an article by D. Jackson, titled 'Artful Dodgers', in *The Weekend Australian* (Jan. 8–9, 2000, p.23). To most people in the IT business, the most likely outcome was a number of relatively minor computer and software glitches in January or February 2000. Nothing like the global meltdown increasingly being forecast. But no-one wanted to listen to these voices of knowledgeable moderation. As Anderson noted: 'Imminent doom sells newspapers: reassurance doesn't'.

Even government ministers were making dire predictions. In November 1998, Australian Senator Ian Campbell released a press statement which ran, in part: 'Even the most advanced organisations in Australia know that it is incredibly unlikely their business will not be affected by the bug'. The following year the Commonwealth Government's Office for Government Online released an expensive free booklet for all citizens titled *Y2K Report: You and the Millennium Bug*. Designed to be reassuring, this thirty-page colour publication aimed to help Australians deal with the millennium bug. It included information on:

* how it might affect your home
* how it might affect services you depended on
* what to do about it
* what rights you have in addressing problems

Now the government had bought into the delusion. Of course, for the reasons mentioned, they had no choice. Nevertheless, the very existence of such outputs from the supposedly credible and authoritative sources of information only served to worsen the hysteria for many.

The third element of significance in the Y2K delusion was the combination of folklore and officialdom. The many ancient fears relating to the end of one millennium and the start of another have their origins in the irrational, and are transmitted especially through informal communication such as word of mouth, and in the apocalyptic publications of some religious fringe groups. When a technological reason for a millennium problem arose and began to be trumpeted through the mainstream media, there was a convergence of folklore and authority that gave the doom scenario a veneer of credibility. The Internet literally exploded with millennial forebodings and prognostications of the most dire and lurid kind, adding fuel to the flames as more and more people came 'online' with the increasingly affordable provision of computers, modems and the necessary software for accessing the Internet and e-mail.

In the event, the whole thing was a gigantic fizzer. Almost nothing happened as the moment of doom ticked by. The previously rabid alarmists back-pedalled rapidly, claiming they had been performing a service for humanity and that it was due to their warnings that government and industry worked together to solve the problem.

The afore mentioned senator wrote an article in which he claimed that Australians had not been taken in by purveyors of Y2K panic and so had enjoyed a trouble-free summer holiday with business as usual. This statement, radically different from that of 1998, appeared in the national newspaper of record a safe six days after apocalypse (*The Australian*, 6 Jan 2000, p.11).

We can make our own interpretations of such expostulations. And of course, the cream of the jest is that we will never really know if they were right or not. Deluded or sceptical, the world is still here at the time of writing, if many billions of dollars worse off.

MANAGE THE DAMAGE

BUSTING BUSINESS LEGENDS AND RUMOURS

These are just a few of the many unofficial communications that continually undermine businesses of all kinds throughout the world. Many others have been documented and studied, as noted in the bibliography.

While it is impossible to quantify the financial damage done by such stories with their negative effect on sales, there is considerable evidence to show that damage to business by rumour, legend and related forms of unofficial communication is large-scale and ongoing. Folklorists, social psychologists, public relations professionals and others have documented such commercial rumours for decades, and there is a sizeable literature available on how to combat the harm that such rumour and legend scares may do.

Where do they come from? Many of these legends and rumours are of considerable age and are simply updated to suit new conditions and products. Why people believe and spread them is a much more difficult question to answer. Most analyses suggest that these stories trade on our uncertainties and suppressed fears about those things over which we have little or no control — the preparation of food in restaurants, what goes on in the boardrooms of large corporations, the consequences of new technology, and so on. Then there is always the possibility of such rumours being deliberately started by groups or individuals with a grudge against a company or its products, or perhaps by competitors. These possibilities are very difficult to establish, though cannot be discounted.

Once the processes of legend development and circulation are understood, various approaches can be taken to combat these outbreaks of commercial hearsay. These could range from community-oriented to full-scale media campaigns. Experience has shown that while commercial rumour and legend outbreaks share many similarities, each new manifestation involves differing circumstances, therefore requiring diagnosis and treatment on an individual basis. However, the following general guidelines may prove helpful.

Firstly, the public should be provided with information that contradicts the essence of the rumour, usually through the mass media. In this approach it is important not to refer to the rumour in any way. Simply supplying authoritative, attractively-produced facts that implicitly refute the rumour may be enough to kill it off.

Another approach is to confine rumour-busting to the area or areas where the rumour is most prevalent. This approach usually leaves out the mass media and concentrates on employees being briefed about the rumour and being given handouts on what to say to customers who believe the rumour to be true. Action of this kind needs to be fast in order to scotch the rumour before it spreads to other localities.

Some experts advocate the head-on confrontation of the rumour through all available channels, including the mass media. This approach is probably only feasible for larger businesses with the necessary resources. As it is generally such 'brand name' businesses that suffer from the more spectacular and damaging rumour scares, this is perhaps an appropriate and effective means of control.

The former R&I Bank in Western Australia successfully used this approach to dampen a rumour of collapse in January 1992. The bank immediately took out full-page advertisements in the newspapers strongly refuting the rumour by stressing the amount of the bank's reserves and their government-backed security. This authoritative and factual rebuttal effectively ended some days of panic withdrawals.

If the 'do nothing' approach fails, a business might consider bringing in a rumour expert to advise on appropriate action. Even the best-intentioned refutations may not achieve the desired result if inadequately prepared and supported. A simple refutation in the press may reinforce the negative elements of the rumour and its consequences.

IF YOU CAN'T BEAT 'EM . . .

Another strategy that applies especially to business and commercial legends could be described as 'if you can't beat 'em join em'. A well-known chain of American department stores, Neiman Marcus, has become the focus for a new version of a hoary urban legend usually known as the 'Red Velvet Cake'. This one usually circulates in the form of a typed or hand-written flyer.

A woman greatly enjoyed a red velvet and white frosted cake served to her at an exclusive hotel in New York. She asked the waiter if he would be so kind as to send her the recipe, and he agreed.

When the recipe duly arrived it came COD with a charge of $300. Outraged, the woman paid up but also consulted her lawyers. They told her there was nothing she could do, so now

she had to get her money's worth by serving the red velvet cake to her friends on special occasions.

The flyer concluded with the recipe for the cake.

The origins of this one go back to the 1930s, but as a legend it has not been documented before the 1950s. The New York hotel, needless to say, denies the legend and has even taken to giving out copies of the recipe to curious inquirers. This may explain why the story migrated to other brands in the early 1980s, and to Neiman Marcus in the 1990s. In this version, which seems to have been massively distributed through the Internet, it is not a cake for which the hapless customers are ripped off, but some excellent cookies. The legend has been updated a little, developed one or two refinements, and now involves credit cards. In confirmation of the proverb that 'familiarity breeds contempt', this one is now so ancient, well known and widespread that it has generated a number of parodies

The point here is that Neiman Marcus has adopted the dual strategy of simultaneously debunking this legend and giving away the cookie recipe to anyone who cares to download it from the company's website. If rebuttals cannot make the legend go away, then at least the company can get some useful PR from the whole thing. And why not? They are also selling the chocolate chip cookies in their in-store cafés.

5

TRAVELLERS' TALES

AUSTRALIANS ARE GREAT travellers, and spend a good deal of time and money overseas. Increasingly we are obtaining information about the places we wish to visit, and how to get there via the Internet. The rapidly evolving communication system of the net is ideal for these purposes, but is also notorious for the transmission of misinformation. One of the largest fields of false belief and hearsay involves one or more aspects of the travel experience. In these much-told travellers' tales, unpleasant things might happen to your home while you are away, dangers are lurking in strange and faraway places, and disasters might befall you while you're getting there.

While these tales are almost always untrue, they are told as credible stories for good reasons: they allow us to express and share fears and tensions about new experiences, they are entertaining, and they usually contain what can be a useful warning or caution. You are likely to hear about the revenge of the airline steward, about hairy-armed hitchhikers, naked caravanners, phantom hitchhikers and hitchhiking nuns prophesying the end of the world, bodies on roofracks, the unusual toilet facilities of the 747 and any amount of such old nonsense.

[IN FLIGHT]

THE AIRLINE STEWARD'S REVENGE

An Australian airline steward was working in First Class on a plane from South Africa to Sydney. A little way into the flight, he approached two of his passengers, a very wealthy and snooty elderly couple. 'What would you like to drink, madam?' he asked.

There was no reply. Thinking that the woman might not have heard him, the steward asked again.

Once again she ignored him, but her husband leaned over and said, 'My wife doesn't speak to the "help". She would like a bottle of red.'

The steward went off to get the wine, but as he walked away the man called out, 'Boy, boy!'

'Yes sir, how can I help you?' asked the steward, returning.

'My wife was wondering about the situation with domestic help in Australia,' said the man.

'Oh sir,' the steward swiftly replied, **'I'm sure madam will have no trouble at all finding a job.'**

According to the union official who told this tale in Sydney in early 1995, the steward was sacked by the airline but later reinstated. There is a very Australian flavour to this one. The story simultaneously puts down the snobbishness of the First Class couple, shows the rapier-sharp wit of the Aussie bloke, and fits in well with our cherished notions of Australia as a place of equality.

THE RESURRECTED CAT

A woman travelling by aeroplane from northern Western Australia to Perth put her cat on the plane as cargo. The aircraft arrived at Perth airport and as the cargo people were unloading they noticed the cat was dead in its little box.

The men were quite disturbed about it, so they went to every cat haven and cat home they knew until they found a cat identical to the one that died.

'That's not my cat!' the woman exclaimed when they delivered the replacement. 'My cat was dead! I was bringing him home to bury him!'

Similar in theme to **The Cat in the Bag** and **Bunny Business** (both in Chapter 3), but a separate tale in its own right, **The Resurrected Cat** is a frequently encountered favourite, told by the general public and also well known in the airline industry.

In *The Mexican Pet*, Jan Brunvand recounts a version of this story involving a poodle flown from Chicago to Rome.

This version has a more dramatic ending — when the owner comes to collect the dog she faints when it jumps out and licks her face.

THE 747 HAS EVERYTHING

A man travelling on a plane urgently needed to use the men's toilet, but the loo door said 'OCCUPIED'. The stewardess suggested that he use the ladies', but cautioned him against pressing any of the buttons on the wall.

Eventually, as he stared at the buttons marked 'WW', 'WA', 'PP' and 'ATR', his curiosity got the better of him. So while sitting there, he carefully pressed the first button marked 'WW'. Immediately warm water sprayed gently over his bottom. 'Golly,' he thought, 'the gals really have it made.'

Now even more curious, he pressed the button marked 'WA' and warm air dried his bottom completely. 'This,' he thought, 'is out of this world.' The button marked 'PP' yielded a large powder puff, which patted his rear end lightly with a scented powder. Naturally, he just couldn't resist the last one marked 'ATR' ...

When he awoke, he was in hospital. He panicked and buzzed for the nurse. 'What has happened? The last thing I remember I was in the Ladies on board a plane.'

'Yes, you were,' replied the nurse, 'but you were told not to touch the buttons. It seems you were having a really great time until you pressed the button marked ATR, which stands for Automatic Tampon Remover. Your penis is under your pillow.'

Another cautionary tale, this time in the form of a piece of photocopy-lore about international air travel. This one seems to have originated in America, but had made it to Sydney by

1989, when it circulated as a 'Christmas Message' — a not-so-gentle reminder of the potential dangers of travel.

Although circulated on paper, the story works just as effectively as an oral tale, and I have heard it told this way in mid-2001. Those inclined towards the Freudian interpretations will no doubt enjoy speculating on the psychoanalytic significance of this yarn, noting the unfortunate fate of the curious traveller, and the fact that he meets it while surrounded by the strange devices that apparently grace the ladies'. Readers may care to compare this story with others that involve the loss of the penis, such as **The Superglue Revenge** (Chapter 2).

[ON THE ROAD]

GRANNY ON THE ROOFRACK

A family took off on their annual holiday, the car packed with Mum, Dad, the kids and Granny. But out in the middle of nowhere on the Nullarbor Plain, Granny died. Distraught and miles from anywhere, the family decided to bundle Gran's body up and lash it to the roofrack. They then drove off in search of the nearest police station to report the death.

Eventually they found the police station and raced inside leaving the car with the body still on the roofrack. When they returned with the sergeant, the car had disappeared. The stolen car and Granny were never recovered.

This is one of the most popular holiday horror stories: like some other modern legends, it has even been incorporated into a number of movies. The situation, as with many other legends, is well and truly ordinary — parents, children and grandmother going on holiday together in the car.

Granny on the Roofrack was the first contemporary legend I heard, or at least the first that I knew *was* a legend. A version of it was told to me in all seriousness by an impeccably spoken English woman in 1978. It had happened to the niece of a friend of hers a few years before while on a motoring holiday on the Continent. The family had been driving across the border at the time. My excited response, as I blurted out something like, 'Oh no, that's a contemporary legend', met with a decidedly cool reception from the storyteller. As far as she was concerned, it was a true story.

Of course, it was old even as long ago as 1978. Folklorist Stewart Sanderson collected a variation of the story, set during the Second World War, in Britain in 1960. He later found a second British version, another in Spain, and even one from Nigeria in 1965. The legend is also known in Scandinavia (probably as early as the 1960s), Switzerland, Italy, Latvia, Germany, Poland, the former Yugoslavia and throughout the United States. It is thought to be derived from eighteenth- and nineteenth-century tales of stolen corpses, or possibly from even earlier European legends.

Many versions of **Granny on the Roofrack** have the grandmother (or aunt) dying just as the family crosses a border of some kind — in the story here it is the considerable physical and psychological 'border' of the Nullarbor Plain. The persistence of this motif, together with the popularity and age of the legend, has led to a good deal of speculation about what it might mean. Theories include the possibility that the story is related to the youth-orientation of contemporary society, with the consequent rejection and disguising of ageing, together with the moving aside of the aged, a view advanced by American folklorist Alan Dundes. Another view, related to the earlier legends, not very convincingly links the story with cannibalism, while yet another theory suggests that the legend is about a universal fear — the return of the dead — which is why Granny is never seen again.

My guess is that the story, at least in its best-known recent versions, has more to do with the peculiarly modern custom of the family automobile holiday — an activity that frequently, easily and quite quickly takes us to out-of-the-way, foreign or otherwise unfamiliar places. The possible dangers of such locations include breaking down in the middle of nowhere, not knowing the local customs and practices in order to summon help, and so on. Most, if not all, of the many renditions of this story have the family overseas or at least far away from their familiar territory. Again, in such circumstances, the apparently normal and ordinary can suddenly turn vicious, with the result that poor Granny has to go up top.

Regardless of these possible explanations, the story turns up in all sorts of guises. Many will be familiar with it in the film *National Lampoon's Vacation*, and a strand of the plot seems to be part of Steinbeck's novel *The Grapes of Wrath*. Bill Scott has a good version, collected in Brisbane in the 1970s, in his *The Long and the Short and the Tall*. Here's another ...

THE CORPSE ON THE CAR ROOF

A young man and his wife were driving the man's aged great-aunt across the Nullarbor Plain to attend a family reunion in Perth in mid-winter. About halfway across the plains Auntie died, and the young wife grew hysterical at the prospect of driving on with a corpse in the car. Her husband, in a fix, removed the luggage from the roofrack, rolled Auntie in the tarpaulin, strapped her to the rack, loaded the luggage into the car and drove on through the dark until they arrived in Albany at three o'clock in the morning. The weather was freezing, and the man was physically and emotionally exhausted, so he decided to report the death to the police first thing in the morning. The couple pulled into a motel, paid for a room and gratefully went to bed, leaving Auntie outside on top of the car.

When they awoke next morning they were horrified to discover that the car had been stolen while they slept, along with Auntie. No trace of the car or the body were ever found.

Again, the travellers are crossing the Nullarbor and an aged passenger dies somewhere out in the desert. Other Australian versions have the incident occurring 'in the Outback' and similarly isolated locations, but the family is always on holiday and driving from somewhere to somewhere far away.

THE WELL-DRESSED ROO

A group of tourists (sometimes Japanese, sometimes American) were being driven through the Outback to see the sights.

When their bus ran down a kangaroo the driver stopped to assess the damage. Excited by this bit of authentic Australiana, the tourists rushed out to have a look. After quite a bit of camera clicking, someone had the bright idea of standing the dead roo up against a tree and putting his sports jacket on the animal for an unusual holiday photograph.

Just as the tourist is about to snap his photo the roo, which was only stunned by the bus, regained consciousness and leapt off into the bush, still wearing the tourist's expensive jacket, which contained his wallet, money, credit cards and passport.

The Well-dressed Roo gives us a chance to have a laugh at the expense of those 'bloody tourists' who have helped to make tourism our fastest-growing industry. Not surprisingly, this tale is an old favourite, and is probably derived from bush yarns about a kangaroo mimicking the actions of humans, especially in relation to arm-lifting at the pub. The story has frequently appeared in the Australian press and local folklorists have collected and published numerous old and new versions of the yarn. In the 1950s the tale was told about visiting English cricket sides and about an Italian America's Cup team in Western Australia. In 1988 Amanda Bishop published a collection of urban legends entitled *The Gucci Kangaroo*, and noted the story as common in Australia.

But the theme of this tale is not unique to Australia — the concept of poetic justice meted out to the humans by supposedly dumb animals has many international variations. There is the American bear that walks off into Yellowstone park carrying a tourist's baby, and the deer hunter who loses his expensive rifle by placing it in the antlers of a deer he has just shot. Like the roo, the deer is only stunned and races off with the weapon still fixed in its horns. Both of these tales are quoted by Jan Brunvand in *The Mexican Pet* (1986), along with a few other Australian versions of **The Well-dressed Roo**. And there are even German versions of the story.

No doubt a group of tourists who attended the 2000 Sydney Olympics have a similar tale to tell; after all, it's too good to be true.

TIME FOR A KIT-KAT

A woman went into a coffee shop and ordered a coffee and a Kit-Kat. The Kit-Kat arrived first, so she put it down on a vacant table and returned to the counter to collect her coffee.

When she returned, a man was sitting at her table eating a Kit-Kat. He'd broken it into four pieces and had already eaten one and started on the second. Outraged, the woman grabbed a wafer of the chocolate bar. The man, looking surprised, moved to the next table and ordered a bun. When it arrived the woman, still angry, moved to his table and ate half of the bun. The man glared at her, got up and left.

Honour and hunger satisfied, the woman went to pay her bill and discovered a Kit-Kat in her bag.

Incorrect assumption is the basis of this story, while the moral is clearly an example of the proverb 'Look before you leap'. Some stories emphasise the age, class or status differences between the man and the woman — in British versions the woman is often older and may be upper-class, even aristocratic. In a mid-1980s New Zealand variation, the man is a punk rocker. **Time for a Kit-Kat** has been around in Britain since at least the early 1970s.

Because no words are exchanged, this incident has the feel — and the appeal — of a Charlie Chaplin skit from the silent movie era. And, as neither are fully described, we are left wondering about the man's puzzlement and the woman's embarrassment. This is a far more subtle approach than the usual 'embarrassing mistake' situations in legends such as **The Surprise Party** in Chapter 2.

THE PHANTOM HITCHHIKER

One dark night, a man was driving his car along a lonely road when all of a sudden the car headlights illuminated the figure of a hitchhiker standing on the roadside. The driver stopped and offered the hitchhiker a lift. Getting into the back seat of the car, the female hitchhiker asked to be taken to an address further down the road. The driver drove on. Arriving at the address she'd given, he pulled over and turned to say goodbye. But the back seat was empty — the hitchhiker had vanished. Puzzled, the driver knocked at the door of the house. An elderly man answered.

'I just picked up a young woman about six miles down the road. She asked to be dropped off at this address, but when I turned round to say goodbye she'd disappeared. Do you know who she could've been?' the driver asked the old man.

Clutching the door frame, the old man burst into tears and, sobbing loudly, explained that the driver had picked up the ghost of his daughter, who'd been killed in a road accident at that spot some years before.

The road is the preferred location for urban legends of the weird and the unexplained. A number of well-travelled tales focus on the theme of disappearance. The most famous of all is **The Phantom Hitchhiker**, also known as 'The Vanishing Hitchhiker' among other titles. It is a classic modern legend that's been around for centuries.

A variation on this one, usually known as 'The Disappearing Driver', reverses the roles of the hitchhiker and the driver. The hitchhiker accepts a lift one dark, stormy night only to be asked by the driver to get out of the car after a short while. The hitchhiker, puzzled, does as he is asked and the car drives away, disappearing into the rainy darkness. He goes to a nearby house, knocks at the door, and tells the residents what has happened. The couple tell him that the man who gave him a lift was killed in an accident at that very spot ten years ago, and ever since it has been known as 'Dead Man's Bend'.

In another vanishing legend, the setting is much the same as for **The Phantom Hitchhiker**, but it is usually a bus rather than a car that is driving through the night. At a particular stop, often near a cemetery, the bus picks up an elderly lady, but when the bus reaches its destination the driver is perplexed to discover that the woman has vanished.

THE FALSE TEETH

A middle-aged couple were holidaying on the Gold Coast. The man loved to swim. One day a big surf was running and he managed to persuade his wife, who was not a keen swimmer, to join him in the water. Not knowing how to handle the waves, the woman was dumped and lost her false teeth. She was pretty upset, so her husband and a couple of other people waded into the sea to search for the dentures. They couldn't find them, but, thinking what a great joke it would be, the man removed his own dentures and handed them to his wife, saying, 'Here darling, we found them'.

His wife washed them in the sea and tried to put them into her mouth. Of course, they didn't fit.

'These aren't my teeth,' she said and, to the husband's horror, threw the dentures far out into the waves.

This well-known holiday yarn is usually set on the Gold Coast, although Sydney's Bondi Beach is sometimes the location. In this 'the biter bit' story the moral is crystal clear — don't play practical jokes, or else.

The tale is also a popular fishing yarn, appearing in fishing publications and anthologies of stories, as well as making the occasional appearance in *Post* magazine. In this version a man loses his dentures over the side of the fishing boat during a bout of seasickness. His practical joker mate takes his own dentures out, ties them to his hook and drops them over the side. After a while he reels in and shows his amazed mate how he has just hooked his teeth out of the briny deep. His mate takes them and has a close look at them. 'Nope,' he says, 'these aren't mine', and tosses them back into the sea.

Bill Scott included this one in his 1985 collection of yarns, *The Long and the Short and the Tall,* and collected an even earlier version which formed part of his 1976 *Complete Book of Australian Folklore.* So, this one has been doing the rounds for a good many years in Australia.

It is also well known internationally and is probably connected to a widespread tale in which a fish, usually a cod, is caught and when opened up is found to have a set of dentures in its gizzards. A couple of Dutch folklorists, Eric Venbrux and Theo Meder, contacted me about this one some years ago. They were writing an impressively learned paper on the origins and meaning of this story and were after Australian versions to add to their catch. The paper was published as 'The False Teeth in the Cod' and shows the ancient origins and very wide diffusion of this slightly discomfiting legend.

THE BABY-NAPPING BIRD

A young couple were holidaying on the coast with their small baby. One lovely day on the beach, the child was crawling happily over the sand when a large bird swept down from the sky, scooped the child up in its beak (alternatively, hooked its claws into the child's nappy) and carried the infant off into the blue.

Don't be ridiculous! What sort of bird could, or would want to carry off a human baby? Such commonsense responses have not stopped this one knocking around Australia and other countries for years. It happened in Kalbarri (Western Australia), on the Gold Coast, in Santa Fe ...

Journalists sometimes are taken in by such stories when they hear them, or when they appear on a wire service or other apparently credible source, such as a fax or computer bulletin board. Dave Hults, a folklorist and keen urban legend detective, heard the story of **The Baby-napping Bird** broadcast on ABC TV news during the summer holiday period in the early 1990s. Knowing that this was a popular international legend, he phoned the ABC for the name of the journalist who had filed the story, contacted him where he was holidaying in the Barrier Reef, and asked him for the source. The journalist said he had heard it from someone while he was dancing with his wife at their hotel. He thought it was a good story and filed it! The ABC TV news desk thought it was a good one, too. In fact, the ABC seems to have fallen in love with this story, and even dramatised the supposed event as part of a documentary about dogs, televised in the mid–90s.

Folklorists have traced versions of this tale back to at least the eighteenth century in Britain and Germany, and it has been noted in many places since then. Sometimes a small pet dog (chihuahuas are the favoured variety) or cat is carried off, rather than a baby, and the bird may be a pelican. Although, an Alaskan bald eagle was reported doing the deed on 19 June 1993, according to an Associated Press news story.

Australian folklorist Bill Scott wrote about this story in his 1996 book *Pelicans and Chihuahuas*. Bill first heard a story from a Canberra Public servant in 1983, in which the chihuahua was eaten by a particularly fearsome tomcat, strategically placed near the poor little doggie by a scheming husband. He included this in his 1985 anthology *The Long and the Short and the Tall*. Late in 1984 he received a clipping from the *Newcastle Herald* in which the chihuahua named 'Pancho' was plucked from the ground by a passing pelican.

From this report, Scott doggedly pursued the legend through the Brisbane *Courier Mail* of 22 August 1985, which reported the chihuahua-napping in Kalbarri, on Bribie Island early in 1986, the UK and Germany in 1988, then back to Australia again. On 20 July 1991 the ABC radio news reported the chihuahua and the pelican story yet again, this time on North Stradbroke Island. It continued to fly in that part of the country, it seems, until picked up by the holidaying ABC journalist.

KID(NEY)NAPPING

A couple of friends went to Los Angeles on a holiday. They went out drinking one evening and teamed up with a few local people. One of the tourists went off with a woman, while his companion returned to the hotel.

The man didn't return for a few days. When he did, he complained of not feeling too well and couldn't remember what had happened. He thought that maybe he'd been drugged and robbed, but he still had his wallet. When he didn't recover his friend looked him over, discovered a cut on his back and took him to a doctor. After various tests, it was found that one of his kidneys had been removed.

Stories such as this, involving an adult who is lured into a situation in which part of the body (usually a kidney) is stolen, are closely related to the rumours about kidnapping and selling children for their vital organs. Folklorist Mark Moravec has made a study of organ kidnap legends and he collected this version in Ballarat, Victoria in 1990.

Such stories have a long history. The current crop seems to originate in South America, where folklorists have traced the tale from early 1987. Claims were made that children were being kidnapped and killed so that their healthy organs could be removed and sent to desperate patients awaiting heart, lung, liver, kidney or other organ transplants in the United States. Different versions of the same tale insist that children in third-world countries are being sold by their parents to body-part traders. Spread by the international media, these stories have since become legends in many countries, including Russia, Italy, Holland and Australia.

This legend has been connected with eighteenth-century stories about children being kidnapped and drained of blood in order to cure the unspecified illness of a French aristocrat. There are also versions in the Netherlands, and the stories may well be linked with age-old fears about the kidnapping and sacrifice of children by evil 'strangers' of various kinds, or by people of non-Christian beliefs. Some of the latest variations involve atrocities in Bosnian prison camps, where prisoners' organs are said to be removed for reuse elsewhere.

Probably the most popular recent version of the kidney-napping yarn is similar to the story related here. A man, travelling with one or more male friends, visits New York (or, less frequently, another American capital city). As in the tale above, they go out one night and the man takes off alone with a woman. He feels 'off colour' the next morning and his friends find a fresh cut on his back. When they take him to a doctor, they discover that one of his kidneys has been removed. An alternative ending is that the friends go up to the victim's hotel room and find him lying semi-conscious in a pool of his own blood.

Other forms of this story circulating in Sydney and Melbourne during the first half of 1995 include the tale of the man who, some years ago, went to India for a holiday. While in Delhi the man became sick and required major surgery. Fortunately, everything went well and he recovered and returned to Australia. A few years later the man needed some minor exploratory surgery and in the process of conducting this, the doctors discovered that the man had only one kidney, the other having been surgically removed.

Then there is the young man who, while holidaying in Bali, had both his kidneys stolen and subsequently died. He lasted for eighteen hours without these vital organs, the loss of which was not discovered until the autopsy. The informant's informant swears that this is a true story.

Not surprisingly, the organ kidnap theme has featured in a number of films. The American film *Coma* (1978) is probably the most familiar to Australian audiences, but German, French and Polish productions have used the same basic idea. A more recent Hollywood mystery film, *The Harvest* (1993), also makes use of the organ kidnap theme.

In Poland, there is a particularly strong tradition of legends involving children being kidnapped for their organs and/or blood by someone in a black car. This theme is echoed in early nineteenth-century European legends, and organ kidnap tales are also known in Russia, in Sicily and throughout mainland Italy. In 1993 the European Parliament heard a speech against the illegal traffic in body parts, and there was a 'stolen organs' abduction scare in Honduras. The October 1993 edition of *Life* magazine contained stories of body-part snatches and the topic has now become an international obsession, even leading to attacks on tourists suspected of organ thefts in Guatemala during 1994.

That was pretty much how things stood with this one back in 1995 when *Granny on the Roofrack* was first published. Since then the stolen kidney legend has evolved in spectacular style. Read on if you dare.

THE GREAT KIDNEY PANIC OF '98

A young man went on holiday to New York. He picked up a woman in a bar, and went back to her place with her. After a wild night of pleasure the young man woke up the following morning naked and sore, sitting in a bath full of splintered ice. As he regained consciousness he noticed the words 'Ring Emergency or die' scrawled on his chest in lipstick. He groggily called the number of the Emergency Services, and they told him to check himself all over for any sign of injury. He did, and discovered two long slits, one on each side of his lower back. When the ambulance arrived, he was informed that his kidneys had been removed, for sale in the spare body-arts trade, which was run by medical students.

This story has grown out of all proportion, and there is even a further rumour that hospitals are putting emergency operating teams on stand-by to deal with the expected influx of kidney-challenged young men.

This basic version of the new kidney story, like the one that got away, has grown out of all proportion over the last few years, cloning itself to the legend about a young man who gets into the same situation, waking alone the next morning to find, scrawled across the bedroom mirror in lipstick, 'Welcome to the world of AIDS' (see Chapter 2). The addition of the medical students' involvement is an update of a nineteenth-century body-snatcher scare. This new version was first noted in North America towards the end of 1996, intensifying through 1997 and still in circulation there in early 1998, around which time it seems to have reached our shores.

Both these stories are expressions of the usually hidden fears that afflict the modern world. Trivial and apparently unbelievable as they are, these fragments of fear have the potential to cause extensive panic and alarm. The current stolen kidney legend has been circulating in Sydney, Melbourne, Brisbane and probably elsewhere, according to a JJJ radio talkback session on Friday 22 May 1998, when callers from all over Australia rang to say that they had heard the kidney legend. Many believed it.

As with all urban myths, the stories they tell are made credible because those who tell them believe them to be true. This is the case with the well-meaning parents and community groups who photocopy the Blue Star Acid flyer, e-mail it, post it on websites and distribute it in church and community newsletters — a widespread hoax documented in Chapter 7. So quickly and widely do these legends and rumours spread that they build a self-justifying climate of belief simply by their existence. Everyone is talking about it, so it must be true.

Often the mass media are implicated, usually unwittingly, in these outbreaks. Urban legends have been published in newspapers and broadcast on radio and TV news as 'true', adding to their credibility. Why did the stolen kidney legend worry us so much in Australia at that particular moment? Without detailed on-the-ground investigation it is difficult to be specific. But a general air of unease related to waterfront industrial confrontations and the beginning of the ongoing Indonesian crisis had filled the press and airwaves for some months. Over a longer period there was, and continues to be, an ongoing concern around Australia about health and medical care, one of the main themes of the kidney legend.

There is also a worldwide trade in body organs that has had considerable exposure over recent years. According to a report in *The Weekend Australian* (28–29 October 1999, p.11), a human kidney could be bought in China for half a million dollars in late 2000. Similarly, human bone marrow was supposedly going for the equivalent of $10,000. Such events and their intensive reporting and analysis can cause a level of non-specific but persistent insecurity, liable to generate urban legend scares.

A journalist covering this story for *The Weekend Australian* of 23–24 January 1999, interviewed Dr John Knight, medical director of the Australian Kidney Foundation. Dr Knight observed that the story cropped up regularly in Australia, and was quoted as saying: 'Of course it's an urban myth. Kidney transplantation involves highly meticulous records. We know where every kidney has come from.'

Ah yes, but where do they go?

The motif of the message scrawled on the mirror with lipstick, or on the wall with blood, is a popular one in urban legendry and can be found in the new versions of the stolen kidney legend and in another creepy legend known as 'The Licked Hand'.

In this one, a young girl keeps her pet dog in the bedroom with her at night. Whenever she wants some reassurance, she puts her hand down bedside the bed and the dog licks it comfortingly. In some versions of the story the girl goes to sleep and when she wakes in the morning the dog is nowhere to be found and scrawled on the wall or mirror are the words 'Humans can lick, too'.

This shocking legend has any number of even more grisly variations. Sometimes the girl is woken by a dripping noise and gets up and goes to the kitchen, thinking the tap is leaking. She goes to the sink to turn it off and discovers a bloody knife. Then she backs into the fridge and realises that the dripping noise is coming from inside. She opens it up to find her butchered dog swinging inside and a note saying 'Humans can lick, too.'

In another, recorded in America in the 1980s, the girl is having a slumber party and it is all her friends who are slaughtered. Other versions feature a blind woman rather than a child or teenager and others involve university students rooming together. This legend also seems to have been well known among British teenagers in the mid to late 1990s.

[FOREIGN PLACES]

THE BALI SPIDERS

A friend of a friend visited Bali for a holiday. While sunning herself on one of the island's beaches, the woman felt a sting on her face and discovered that a small spider had bitten her.

She was a little concerned, but as there seemed to be no immediate effects, she soon forgot all about it and continued to enjoy her holiday.

On her return home she noticed that a small blister had developed on her face where the spider had bitten her. It grew bigger, and she rubbed it until it burst. A host of baby spiders crawled out.

Sometimes the swollen lump bursts on the way back home; in some versions 'thousands' of baby spiders crawl out; sometimes it didn't happen in Bali at all, but in Thailand, Penang or somewhere else exotic and far away.

This is the most common Australian version of a contemporary fable, and was published this way in *Granny on the Roofrack*. But the story has been around for at least twenty years in America and Europe in the following versions.

TRAVEL BUGS

A woman decided to holiday in the Central American country of Guatemala. Part of the holiday included a trek through the jungle, which included spending the night in a tent beneath the rainforest canopy. She had a great time, but on arriving home to the States, noticed that the tiny bite she had sustained on her cheek during the jungle trek was itchy, and it looked a little red. She applied some antiseptic cream to it and went to bed. But when she woke the next morning the bite had grown much larger, and was unbearably itchy. Unable to stop herself, she scratched at the large red mass until it burst, and dozens of tiny spiders crawled out all over her face.

This is but one of many permutations of a well-travelled tale in which the details of the woman traveller (rarely a man), the foreign location and the unpleasant ending change little. But everything else about the tale can vary, and usually does. For instance, according to some tellings the woman is English, Australian, or Scottish, and her holiday destination is Africa, South America, Bali, India, Mexico, Thailand, Penang or Spain.

In some versions of this story, the woman visits a doctor when she returns home and the medic lances the blister, freeing all the baby spiders. Sometimes the poor woman is so horrified by what is happening to her that she has a heart attack or goes raving mad.

A similar tale was told in Norway during the 1970s and was even picked up as a 'true' story by the Norwegian media in 1980. Its appeal, if it can be called that, is based upon the fear of bodily invasion by a foreign object or species (see **The Tapeworm** and **The Redbacks in the Dreadlocks** for some other examples of this favourite urban legend theme). In this tale, that fear is allied with the fear of exotic locations and the possible dangers that one might, ahem, face there.

This story began to circulate in Australia in the early 1980s, as the Indonesian island of Bali was opened up to tourism. The more widespread version of this story usually involves earwigs and is related to the tale of **The Bouffant Hairdo** discussed in Chapter 3.

In the versions just mentioned, this story has been on our lips, in the media and on the Internet since at least 1980 and according to some sources, since the middle of the 1960s. But the story may well be older than that. It has been compared with an 1842 short story by Jeremias Gotthelf, titled *Die Schwarze Spinne*. In this story, a woman makes a pact with the devil, who kisses her on the cheek to seal the deal. But the devil is cheated by the other villagers, and the spot on the woman's cheek where the devil kissed her swells up and eventually bursts. Of course, lots of poisonous spiders come crawling out.

As with many modern myths, this tale has featured in films, including *Bliss* (1985), *The Nature of the Beast* (1987) and *The Believers* (1987). Versions are also found in the media, including London's *Daily Telegraph* on 12 March and 14 April 1988. The Norwegian media ran with the spiders in 1980 and it has been collected by folklorists all over the world. According to American urban legend scholar Jan Brunvand, this story first came to light in its modern form in Britain and northern Europe in 1980. The victim was usually said to have been holidaying in the south of Europe or in North Africa. Since then, the story has become one of the most frequently told travel myths, playing as it does on our lingering suspicions about foreign places and the things that just might happen to you if you travel to them.

Applying the credibility test to **The Bali Spiders** and its international variations: spiders do not lay their eggs in, or on, people, and although there are some other insects who just might, they don't do it by biting you. There are also similar horror legends involving ants, cockroaches and other nasties infecting human body cavities, or nesting under plaster-casts. But don't worry, these are not travel myths.

TRAVELLERS' CAUTION

The urban legendry of travelling is full of misadventures, hazards, disasters and dire warnings of what might go wrong. A whole book could be compiled of these travel legends, and probably should be, as some of the advice contained in the stories is useful common sense. Here's a round-up of a few of the diverse but worrying tales of travel that you just might hear as you plan your next holiday.

There is the oft-told tale about the horrified passengers of an in-flight jumbo witnessing the pilot who has locked himself out of the cockpit trying to force his way back with an axe. This might be accompanied by the story of someone firing a bullet through the plane wall, causing everything inside to be sucked out through the small hole.

Or you might come across a tale that has been in circulation since at least the late 1940s. Known as 'The Bedbug Letter', it tells of a traveller who is bitten by insects while travelling by plane. He complains to the airline, and some days later receives a most apologetic letter from the company offering him a free upgrade on his next flight. As he goes to dispose of the envelope he notices a yellow Post-it note, with the words 'Just send this clown the standard bedbug letter'.

Oh, and ladies, please refrain from wearing inflatable bras while travelling by air. They have a tendency to inflate and explode due to changes in cabin pressure.

The dreadful things that might happen to you while you are away are almost infinite. You can be abducted at Disneyland, attacked by Greek vampires or bitten by snakes in any number of amusement parks. If you're travelling in Europe, you might get advance notice of the end of the world from the creepy nuns who give you a lift in their battered old rattler. If you are travelling in Australia, beware of bunyips, yowies and those north Queensland yaramas. If you're going further afield, watch out for the Bali spiders and any number of other travel bugs. And spare a thought for the bloke who has been waiting for his flight at Paris airport for ten years. Apparently this is true, even though it sounds like an urban legend.

If you should happen to be mistakenly picked up by the police in a foreign location for streetwalking, relax. You just need to pay a fine and they will issue you with a licence for prostitution. Hey, it's got to be better than going to one of those foreign gaols, right? This one has been with us since at least the mid–1960s.

Things that just might happen back home while you are off sunning yourself in some exotic resort are comprehensively covered in all those burglary stories, and the girlfriend's alfalfa revenge. If you're a male air traveller and have been taking advantage of the airline's policy of flying wives for free, watch out for that incriminating letter from the airline when you get home. You know, the one addressed to your wife that asks her how she enjoyed her trip with you to last month's conference. The one you told her not to worry about, as it would just be boring for her.

All in all, travelling is a pretty hazardous undertaking at the best of times. But then, according to urban mythology, even worse things can happen to you at home. The dunny can explode with you on it. There are burglars who might do unspeakable things with your toothbrush (see **Photographic Evidence**), crazed baby-sitters are itching to cook your baby in the microwave and there are armies of druggies peddling Blue Star Acid. All the worry is enough to make you want to take a holiday.

BACK HOME

A HOLIDAY WIN

A couple's phone rang one day. An excited man on the other end told them that they had just won a week's holiday for two in Bali. 'But you'll need to pack quickly,' he said, 'because you're off tomorrow! The tickets are waiting for you at the airport.'

Thrilled and excited, the couple packed their bags, and early next morning they caught a taxi out to the airport. Sure enough, the tickets were there and their plane duly jetted off to the romantic and exotic location. They had a wonderful holiday: surfing, snorkelling, walking along the sandy beaches and generally relaxing.

When the week was up the couple reluctantly returned from their holiday, tanned, refreshed and very pleased with their good luck. But when they reached their home they were horrified to discover the front door smashed and the house completely stripped by burglars. They'd taken the lot. The holiday 'win', of course, was a ploy to lure them away from the house so that the robbers could plunder with impunity.

As a number of tales in this chapter suggest, holidays can be dangerous things to take. This suspicion is confirmed in this fable, the moral of which is *always* look a gift horse in the mouth. This story is also related to the group of tales that deal with burglary, especially **Tickets to a Show**, and others in Chapter 6.

PHOTOGRAPHIC EVIDENCE

In the early hours of the morning a young married couple returned home after a night out on the town to find that their home had been burgled. Everything of value was gone: the TV, the stereo, the jewellery — even the furniture.

While the husband rang the police, the woman tried to ascertain what exactly had been stolen. It was devastating! They'd been cleaned out — there seemed to be nothing of any value left. About the only thing the burglars left was the couple's camera which, oddly, they discovered in the bathroom as they unhappily cleaned their teeth before going to bed.

Some months later, the couple finished off the roll of film that had been in the camera when the burglars struck. But when they collected the prints they were horrified to find pictures, early on in the roll, of two young men — clearly the burglars — cleaning their behinds with the couple's toothbrushes!

Photographic Evidence is another burglary story, with more than a touch of the 'dreadful contamination' theme. Some versions had photographs of burglars cleaning the toilet bowl, rather than their rear ends, with the toothbrushes.

In recent versions of **Photographic Evidence** the protagonists are tourists, whose clothes and other belongings are stolen from their suitcases or backpacks while their camera is apparently left untouched. The tourists continue with their holiday and then return home a few weeks later. When their holiday snaps are developed, they discover, very early in the roll, a photo of the thieves using their toothbrushes in one of the nastily unpleasant ways described.

Although **Photographic Evidence** is popular in Australia, we can't claim to have originated this one either, at least not on the evidence. In his 1978 collection of urban legends, *The Tumour in the Whale*, Rodney Dale recounts a published version called 'The Final Curtain'. Set in Surrey, the unlucky home owners were given tickets to the theatre by the cunning burglar, who then proceeded to make unconscionable use of their toothbrushes. Dale also writes that the story was told to him twice, presumably around the mid-1970s. From at least the early 1970s, Scandinanvian folklorists have been reporting this story, which is often set in Oslo, Norway.

THE GNOMES ARE BACK!

In *Granny on the Roofrack* I reported on a severe rash of gnome-napping and related disappearances (pink flamingos, garden rabbits — you know, the standard stuff) that plagued the country in the 1980s and early 1990s. Those colourful garden gnomes were vanishing almost daily from gardens, porches and patios across the nation. Sometimes they would send a postcard from exotic holiday locations, or perhaps a photograph of them sunbathing on a distant beach resort would turn up in the post. More ominously, some gnomes had not left of their own accord, but had been abducted and were the subject of ransom demands. Usually, just as mysteriously as they had disappeared, the gnomes would reappear in their garden niche as if nothing untoward had occurred, often complete with travel bags.

The last gnome-napping report I had found at that stage

was from the late 1980s. I thought the madness must have faded. But just when you think an urban legend has finally died away, it sneaks back up on you ...

Imagine my horror when I opened up the *Weekend Australian* of 13–14 October 2000 to find smirking on the front cover a gnome, accompanied by the headline 'Gnome and Away'.

Inside I learned that the journos at the magazine had been visited by the gnome pictured, but the poor little fella had been almost immediately abducted. A note demanding ransom for his safe return duly arrived and 'needless to say we paid up, and the gnome duly reappeared', wrote editor Candida Baker, obviously greatly relieved.

So, the gnomes are back — briefly. Look out for them around your way, they're hard to miss. If you cannot find any actual gnomes, they are leading a busy life on the web. Try: **members.aol.com/gnomeweb/gnomehome.htm** if you really must.

6

CRIMINAL ACTIVITIES

C RIMINAL BEHAVIOUR, real and imagined, is an especially fertile seedbed for the growth of urban legends in Australia and the rest of the world. The favoured themes of crime-lore are varied.

One of the most frequent involves illicit drugs — their effects, abuse and distribution, a topic also covered in Chapter 7 with the **Blue Star Acid** hoax. As with most urban legendry, drug crime tales get bigger and bigger in the telling. For instance, we have developed an interesting body of drug-related beliefs and half-truths around the unattractive creature known as the cane toad.

Penetration of the home by unwanted visitors of one kind or another also remains a common theme of contemporary crime legends, as do fears about what might happen to you in everyday locations such as in automobiles or at the shops. However, even while urban legends may frighten many of us, they also provide a few (admittedly not many) compensations in which the wronged get their revenge and the criminal get their just desserts. But even in these items of not-very-warm comfort there is usually a twist to the tale.

[DRUGS]

THE USED SYRINGES

One of the major concerns of contemporary life is the use and abuse of drugs. This ranges from the everyday abuse of over-the-counter cough medicines to narcotics addiction. As well as causing personal and family misery to thousands, the drug issue permeates many other aspects of Australian life, including crime, social work, politics and health care. Considerable resources of all kinds are devoted to 'fighting' or otherwise dealing with drug use and abuse. The media has taken a lively interest in the more sensational aspects of what is undoubtedly a very real and pressing problem.

As a result of all this, and combined with what is still widespread public ignorance about drug-taking, there is a great deal of tension in the community about drugs and related issues. This makes the subject an ideal urban legends topic. Nowhere is the subject of drug-taking more sensitive than its impact — real or feared — on children. We continually hear stories about junkies deliberately leaving their used needles point-upwards in and around primary schools or other places where children congregate.

While this unfounded paranoia is related to the AIDS scare, it also stereotypes drug users as callous fiends out to harm our children simply for the sake of it. Most drug users are still caring human beings, and many are parents themselves. Some are not, but the same goes for non-drug users. This reality, though, like many others, does not get a look-in when the subject of drugs and children is concerned. The following item and the **Blue Star Acid** saga in Chapter 7 demonstrate this only too well.

The upturned syringe story is also an update of earlier, and still current, beliefs that people ill-disposed towards children were placing razor blades or cut glass on slippery-dips in parks and playgrounds.

THE CANE TOAD HIGH

'Turning on With Toads a Turn-Off' went the headline of an article in *The Weekend Australian* of 27–28 February 1999. The article examined the truth behind claims that it was possible to get high on cane toads. It seems that the Queensland police had issued a warning about this practice, as the wet season was filling the backyards of north Queensland with the little beasts. The police were worried that this would tempt Queenslanders to take part in dangerous experiments involving toads. There was some difference of opinion about whether a cane toad high was best obtained by smoking the dried skins, making cane toad soup or simply by licking the ugly brutes.

The journalist, Kevin Meade, set out to discover the truth. He interviewed a number of experts and quoted Professor

Ross Alford of James Cook University, who had met an ageing hippie who claimed to have tried it. Another cane toad expert at James Cook, Di Barton, was quoted in support of this claim. She added the intriguing clue that the last time she'd heard about it was in the late 1980s, when an episode of the then-popular TV series 'LA Law' had featured someone addicted to licking the skins of live frogs.

Anyway, whether you can get high or not from these practices, the belief that you can has been around for quite a while. An article in *Scientific American* in August 1990 implied that cane toad licking inspired the 'drug-war hysteria in the US'.

In his 1993 urban legend book, *The Baby Train*, Jan Brunvand suggests that this all stems from 1950s medical experiments on the psycho-active properties of bufotenine, the substance cane toads secrete from their glands. The United States Drug Enforcement Agency (DEA) banned bufotenine in the late 1960s after experimental subjects experienced negative side effects, which seems to have encouraged a few people to give the cane toads a try. In the mid-1980s media stories began appearing about cane toad abuse, using headlines like 'Toads Take a Licking from Desperate Druggies', inspiring some teenagers to 'suck it and see'.

Apart from the 'yuk factor' involved in licking the loathsome-looking cane toads, the effects are not very ecstatic according to Professor Alford. He explained that your heart will get out of sync, which could lead to paralysis and seizures, salivating and vomiting. Also, the lack of oxygen in your blood will 'turn you blue'. Professor Alford also said: 'Other likely effects are respiratory failure and death'. Oh.

Long before anyone thought of taking a lick on a toad, cane or otherwise, the loathsome little creatures were celebrated or blamed for all manner of things. In the seventeenth century toads were powdered for medical purposes, including drawing contagion from the air. The poison of a toad was thought to assist with plague blisters, and dried toad soaked in vinegar would stop a nosebleed. Toads, usually sliced or diced in various unpleasant ways, were used to cure a variety of afflictions, from sprained wrists to small-pox, unsuccessfully in the latter case. They were also variously thought to be either good or bad luck, and were associated with witchcraft. Possession of a toadstone, actually a bone extracted from the head of a toad, was thought to be useful in warding off assorted evils, and to repulse poisons.

As well as all the medicinal uses, it is believed that toads can live for a great many years without food or water. There are many stories of toads entombed in trees, stone, and concrete, for hundreds of years and then coming out alive.

With the clammy feel of toadskin and their bilious appearance, toads were destined to be losers from the first.

[INVASIONS OF PRIVACY]

TICKETS TO A SHOW

A man parked his car in the driveway one night, and woke in the morning to the sounds of a thief driving off in his car! He notified the police, but a few days later the car was returned to

its original position, completely undamaged, with a note on the dash that said: 'Apologies for stealing the car, I desperately needed to borrow it. Note I've filled the tank. Please find enclosed two tickets to (a show that was on in Perth) . . . '

The man notified the police that the car had been returned, and went to the show. But while he was there, his house was burgled: a removal van backed up and took everything. Neighbours saw it and just assumed he was moving.

Penetration of the family home by burglars is a favourite theme of contemporary legends. Usually there is a bizarre twist (see **Photographic Evidence**) or grotesque element (**The Bloody Burglar**) in the plot. In **Tickets to a Show** the apparent remorse of the thief sets the scene for a twist that hits us in our insecurities.

According to the *Sydney Morning Herald*'s 'Stay in Touch' column of 21 September 1987, Agence France-Presse news service reported a family in Treviso, Italy, that suffered much the same experience — although, in this case, the tickets for two were for a booking at a restaurant for the whole family. The editor of the column identified this as 'a very old Italian urban myth'. But when the story reached Perth in early October, it appeared without comment in *All About Town*.

We might be tempted to think that an urban legend had been traced to its source. But no. In April 1987, five months before the French news service placed the story onto the international news network, the tale above was told by a forty-eight-year-old Perth man who said he heard it first in the early 1980s.

This story and its variations has remained a favourite of modern hearsay, being collected in Britain, America, Canada, Spain and Norway. In America it is sometimes combined with another legend known as 'The Robber Who

Was Hurt'. In this one a woman is home alone, usually doing the ironing when a male hand comes in through a partly-open window, in an attempt to unlock it and enter the house. The woman promptly places the red-hot iron on the hand. There is a scream and the hand is rapidly withdrawn. After a few minutes the woman goes next-door to tell the neighbours what has happened. There she finds her neighbour's husband bandaging a severely burned hand.

As a number of folklorists have pointed out, this is an update of a very old story theme which exists as a fairy tale known as 'The Clever Maid at Home Kills the Robbers'. It is also found in an even older legend involving a witch who takes the shape of a black cat or dog to do someone damage. The victim fights back, severely injuring the attacking animal's paw. Later, back in human form, the witch is revealed when she is found with a wounded hand. Usually she comes to a rather nasty end at the hands of the outraged community.

IS ANYBODY HOME?

A woman was at home alone one day, cleaning the house, when there was a knock at the door. She opened it to find a tall, large woman smiling at the doorstep, who asked to come in and show her some products.

The woman invited the visitor inside, and she then went through the rigmarole of explaining the properties of her products, but she didn't make a sale.

Before leaving, the visitor asked to use the toilet and the woman directed her down the hall. Minutes passed and still she hadn't emerged from the toilet when the woman heard her calling out for more toilet paper. Having just topped up the toilet paper holder she immediately became suspicious and called the police. Terrified, she then locked herself in a cupboard. When the police arrived they ran into the bathroom and found a man waiting there, totally naked.

Is Anybody Home? is another legend that deals with the invasion of the privacy and security of the home. The idea of a man lurking within the presumed safety of the home while a woman is there alone is an ominous and potent one. The element of a man gaining entry to the home dressed as a woman is also frightening and appears again in **The Lady with Hairy Arms** (Chapter 6), where it imparts a similar, additional chill.

THE FAITHFUL HOUND

A young couple who had recently become parents for the first time suddenly found that they had to rush out to attend an emergency. Not having had time to arrange a babysitter, they put their trust in the faithful family dog to look after their young baby. Leaving the baby in its cot, they locked the dog in the house and dashed off.

On returning home, they rushed in to check on the baby. When they turned on the bedroom light, they were greeted by the sight of their faithful hound slavering over blood and flesh on the carpet. Their baby was nowhere to be found. Obviously, their faithful hound had killed the baby! Stricken with guilt and horror, the young parents immediately killed the dog by slashing its throat.

Just as this execution was completed, the parents heard a whimpering sound. Desperately scouring the room, they traced the source of the sound to beneath the baby's cot. There was the baby, alive and well, beside the body of a German shepherd.

Bewildered and relieved, the parents hugged and kissed their child as the police burst in. 'Have you seen a German shepherd round here?' asked the police sergeant. 'We're tracking down a mad one that's taken to attacking children.'

The couple were horrified: their faithful hound that they had just killed had torn the German shepherd to pieces to protect the baby.

The legend of **The Faithful Hound** has been traced to the medieval period in the Welsh tale of Prince Llewellyn's loyal dog. In this earlier story, Prince Llewellyn went out hunting without his hound, Gellert, as he could not find the dog anywhere in the castle. The hunt was not a success and Llewellyn returned in great anger. As he approached the castle, Gellert came bounding towards him with blood dripping from his fangs. This strange sight caused the prince to rush to his small son's nursery, where Gellert and the boy often played together. When Llewellyn reached the nursery, he found blood spattered all around, the cot upturned and no sign of his son. Believing that the hound had killed and eaten the boy, Llewellyn drew his sword and killed Gellert. Just as he did, there was a small cry from underneath the cot — it was his son, just waking up and unharmed. Lying next to the child was the torn and bloody remains of a wolf. Gellert had obviously defended the sleeping child by slaying the beast. Deep in grief and guilt, Llewellyn buried Gellert with great ceremony, covering the grave with a cairn of stones. The place of the burial is called *Beth Gellert*, meaning the grave of Gellert.

In India it is a mongoose that saves the child and is unjustly despatched. In Japan a story about the twelfth-century warrior hero Tametomo involves his pet dog, which suddenly jumped at the volatile warrior one day. Irritated, Tametomo whipped out his sword and sliced off the dog's head. As the head flew into the air, the dog's teeth attached themselves to a giant snake hanging from the tree above, about to attack the hero. Tametomo was very sorry for what he had done and buried the dog respectfully.

The modern form of the story, with its double-edged moral concerning the invasion of privacy and the danger of jumping to conclusions, is well known elsewhere in the world and has been linked to another faithful dog legend, dubbed 'The Choking Doberman' by Jan Brunvand.

THE BLOODY BURGLAR

A woman came home to find her dog choking in the hallway. She rushed it to the local vet who said the dog had something caught in its throat — it would require urgent surgery and need to stay in overnight.

The woman returned home. As she opened the front door the phone rang. It was the vet. 'Get out of the house,' he ordered her, 'and go to the next-door neighbours'. I've rung the police and they're on their way to your house. Go now!'

Impressed and frightened by the vet's tone of voice, the woman dropped the phone and rushed out of the house to the neighbours. Almost immediately the police arrived and burst in. A few minutes later they came out dragging a terrified burglar they'd found whimpering in a cupboard, with two fingers of his right hand bitten off.

A version of **The Bloody Burglar**, set in Ferntree Gully, Victoria, featured in The *Sydney Morning Herald*'s 'Column 8' during 1984. There are other well-known versions of the story in which the burglar is so badly savaged by the guard dog that he dies from blood loss. When the owners return home they discover the burglar's corpse on top of the wardrobe, where he climbed to escape the beast below.

In other versions of this unsettling tale the woman finds the bloody burglar cowering in a cupboard before the vet rings. Sometimes there is a trail of blood leading to the burglar's hiding place. In another version, the burglar has long gone, but the police are able to track him down by taking prints from the severed fingers.

LOST PROPERTY, PROPERTY LOST

A Sydney woman went to the ladies' toilets in a department store. She hung her handbag on the hook near the top of the cubicle door and someone reached over the top of the door and took her handbag while she was sitting on the toilet.

The next day she received a phone call from the lost property department of the store, telling her that her handbag had been handed in. She went to the store straightaway, but when she got there, none of the staff had ever heard of her or the handbag. So she went home and found that the house had been burgled. The thief had got her address and phone number from her bag, called and pretended to be the store to get her out of the house, then robbed it while she was away.

Pauline Bryant was told this tale about the famous Sydney retail store in the late 1950s. She was moving from the country to the city, and her parents told their children this tale to alert them to the dangers of city living.

Generally known as 'The Double Theft', this one was documented by folklorists in England as early as 1972. Since then the tale has been told around the world in Canada, Italy, Spain, Norway and throughout the United States.

[VEHICULAR VIOLENCE]

THE KILLER IN THE BACK SEAT

When driving alone along the freeway very late one night, a woman noticed a car flashing its high-beam in her rear-vision mirror. She couldn't understand what was going on and became increasingly frightened, driving faster and faster to get away. But the car continued to follow her and flash its lights.

Eventually she reached her home and screeched into the driveway. The car followed her up the driveway, and in a real panic, she leant on the horn, waking her husband, who came running out as the driver of the other car walked towards her.

'What's going on?' the husband yelled. The other guy pulled open the back door of the car and revealed a man hiding in there with a very big axe.

It turned out that the other driver had been going to work and, as he swung onto the freeway behind the woman, had seen the silhouette of the man in the back seat of the car.

The Killer in the Back Seat seems to have surfaced in the United States during the 1960s, and I have vague memories of the story being told to me around that time in Australia. In some versions the car overtakes the woman and the driver rolls the window down and commands her to drive behind him and do exactly what he does. She follows the car, which speeds and skids erratically along the road, until a man with an axe, perched on the roof of her car, is dislodged. In other stories a service-station attendant spots the killer and, by some ruse, gets the woman out of the car, whereupon the police are called.

When I included this legend in *Granny on the Roofrack* I hadn't heard it for quite a while. But then it featured in the 1998 teen slasher flick *Urban Legend*, which gave it a whole new lease of life. It is closely related to **The Lady with Hairy Arms** and the other scare legends included in this section. These legends are frequently invoked in situations where serial killers and other predators terrorise a community without being caught.

THE HOOK

Late at night a woman was driving through a lonely part of the city and saw a man hitchhiking. Concerned for someone being out there alone so late, she pulled up to offer him a lift. As the

hitchhiker reached for the door handle, the woman noticed that he had a glistening metal hook where his right hand should be. In a panic, she put her foot down and screeched off to the nearest police station. On arrival, she was shocked to see a metal hook attached to the bloody stump of an arm hanging from the door handle.

Horrible. Sometimes there is no hook in the story — just a hairy hand or a few grisly fingers hanging on the door — but the message is the same.

I first heard this story in Leeds, England, in 1977–78. It was widely told at that time, possibly in response to the fears about the 'Yorkshire Ripper', who had been murdering women in and around the Leeds area for years. The police had been unable to capture the killer and the community was very, very nervous. This tale was picked up by the local media and was even broadcast on television news bulletins.

The legend continues to feature frequently in studies of United Kingdom teenage children's traditions, although recently-published research suggests that its popularity has been overtaken by **The Head** in adolescent storytelling. In particular, research has been carried out on the popularity of the story in relation to community panics related to murderers. In America there was a marked increase in the circulation of the legend during the late 1950s and early 1960s in response to the Caryl Chessman case. In Britain, the legend had another upsurge focusing on the figure of Frank Mitchell, 'The Mad Axeman', a notorious violent criminal who escaped from Dartmoor Prison in December 1966.

The Hook is another 'modern' legend that has had a thorough going-over by folklorists of many persuasions — historical, psychoanalytical and sociological. While they don't agree on much, their interest, together with the extreme popularity and diffusion of the story, indicates its importance in the modern psyche. In Australia, however, it seems that this legend is most popular in the form known as **The Severed Fingers.**

A HAIRY HITCHHIKER

A lone woman driver picked up a female hitchhiker, who climbed into the back seat of the car. It was not until they had gone a kilometre or so that the driver noticed, through the rear-vision mirror, that the woman's hands were very hairy. The worried driver decided to stop the car on the pretence of having a blowout, and convinced the hairy hitchhiker to get out to help her change the tyre.

As soon as the hitchhiker got out of the car, the woman jumped back in and drove off at speed to the nearest police station. On arriving in a distraught state, she reported what had happened. The sceptical police sergeant superciliously examined the car. Lying on the back seat was an axe.

Many, many variations of this story have been reported. A favourite version with American teenagers since the 1950s involves a young couple making love in an isolated location. An announcement comes over the car radio that a maniac has escaped from the local asylum. The girl becomes frightened and asks the boy to take her home. Frustrated, but obliging, the boy plants his foot on the accelerator and roars home. When they get to the girl's house they find a bloody hook hanging from the car door handle.

While these tales are apparently of the here and now, they

also have historical precedents. British folklorists have identified a man in women's clothing leaving behind a brace of loaded pistols in a horse-drawn coach in the 1830s, and American research has found mid to late nineteenth-century versions.

GIRLS!!! BEWARE!!!

This appeared in *The Sydney Morning Herald*'s Column 8 on 17 January 1998. The item began: 'Do we have a new urban myth actually starting in Sydney? Doing the rounds of Hurstville shops and offices is a notice':

GIRLS!!! BEWARE!!!
A woman parked her car in the car park to find upon her return that the window had been smashed. A man appeared from nowhere, claiming his car has been stolen, and asked the woman for a lift to the nearest police station, so they could report it together.

She said she was going to let the security guard know first, but he kept trying to push her for a lift. She stood her ground and went and found the security guard. When the security guard and the woman came back to the car the man was gone. Upon checking the car, they found a rope and knife, which had been planted under the passenger seat.

This allegedly happened in the car park at Westfields Hurstville, but when the *Herald*'s journalists checked with the local police, they had heard nothing about the incident. However, reporters on the local paper, the Bankstown

Torch, knew all about it. Variations of the report had the incident occurring in Padstow, Caringbah, Camden and Campbelltown.

This supposedly happened at countless locations in the USA, Britain, Europe and elsewhere in Australia. In the case of this particular version of the legend, it is the unaccompanied woman's fear of male malignity that is being played on.

THE LADY WITH HAIRY ARMS

While out shopping, a woman was approached by an elderly lady who said, 'Excuse me, dear, I'm not feeling too well. Could I trouble you for a lift to my doctor? He's only just a little way down the road.'

Full of sympathy, the younger woman helped the elderly lady to the car, eased her into the front passenger seat and deposited her shopping bag in the back. She was about to drive off when she noticed that the elderly woman had unusually hairy arms. Realising that her passenger was actually a man in women's clothes, the woman jumped from the car and rushed to the shopping centre manager's office to relate her frightening experience and call the police.

When the police arrived they accompanied the woman back to her car. Of course, the woman with hairy arms had gone, but she had left her shopping bag in the back seat. When the police opened it they found an axe inside.

This rumour scare was reported in the Perth newspapers during 1988, accompanied by authoritative police statements that no such event had occurred. The story spread rapidly, however, and created a degree of panic in the local community, which was being terrorised by 'the south-side rapist' at the time.

The Lady with Hairy Arms turned up in Melbourne and Sydney and is still heard from time to time — reported from a friend who heard it from another friend to whom it happened.

The story, however, predates the south-side rapist by many years. A version from the early 1970s told exactly the same tale, the only difference being that it happened in another Perth suburb altogether. A student investigating urban legends remembered where and when she had first heard this yarn, and went back to the neighbour who had originally told her the tale. The neighbour was under the impression that the shopper was indeed axed to death by the lady with hairy arms, but was no longer too clear about the details. The student then went to the local police to request details — their records did not go back that far, but no-one could remember the incident. If such an event had actually taken place, it seems most unlikely that everyone would have forgotten about it.

┌ ABDUCTIONS AND
CASTRATIONS ┐

THE BABY SNATCHER

On the afternoon of Wednesday 16 March 1994, while his mother waited at a supermarket counter, a seven-month-old child was the victim of an attempted abduction at the Dog Swamp Shopping Centre in suburban Perth. The mother turned around to see a man wheeling the child's pram away, but when she shouted at the man and pursued him, he abandoned the pram and ran off.

News of the incident was broadcast on Perth radio. People told their friends about it. Television news crews arrived at the Dog Swamp Shopping Centre, but they were only able to film a puzzled representative of the centre management, who knew nothing of the abduction. The centre was quiet at the time, yet people in nearby shops and offices saw and heard nothing unusual, and the incident was not reported to the centre's management. Despite the fact that there were no witnesses and the mother and baby disappeared, police were said to be searching for a grey-haired man in his fifties.

A similar rumour scare moved rapidly around the United States in the early 1990s. The basic story was that, while at a local shopping centre, a mother discovered that her young daughter was missing. The manager was alerted, the store locked and searched thoroughly, and the little girl was finally located in the women's rest room, accompanied by a woman who had cut the child's hair and dressed her as a boy.

This rumour was reported in various versions throughout southern Louisiana, Texas, New England and many other parts of the country. Some variations of the story of this rumour, which has also been documented in a 1930s form in New Zealand, had the young girl drugged and about to be carried off to the white slave trade. The various police forces in the communities where the rumour circulated were unable to confirm that any such incidents had occurred, but stories still generally persisted for some months.

There is nothing new about these rumours or legends — I remember being told of similar things in Australia during the 1960s. Jan Brunvand has treated this story and its variations in his collections of contemporary legends and rumours, *The Vanishing Hitchhiker* (1981) and *The Choking Doberman* (1986), as have other folklorists. It was known in America in the early 1970s and is just one of a number of stories about the dangers of shopping.

These legends are similar to often-heard tales about young girls being kidnapped in public places (usually from public toilets) — as in **White Slavers in the Loo.**

WHITE SLAVERS IN THE LOO

'You know how some young girls disappear and nothing's ever heard of them again? Well, rumour has it that there was a black market thing going on in the eastern states, where the girls were offered well-paid work in nightclubs, but were instead trapped in harems in Saudi Arabia. Most of them never came back.'

This version of the story is perhaps the 'soft option', avoiding the direct suggestion of forced prostitution. In most versions the motivation offered for the abductions is that the girls are to be sold into the white slave trade, variously located in Saudi Arabia or, more recently, Southeast Asia. An even worse destination is Canberra ...

SHANGHAIED TO CANBERRA

'Girls would go to public toilets in the shopping centres, and they'd be drugged by gangs and dragged out. It happened to a friend of mine who went to the toilet by herself while her mum was shopping nearby, but luckily her mum saw them dragging her out and raised the alarm and she got away. They would take the girls to the outskirts of Canberra for prostitution rings there.'

This West Australian version, referring to alleged events in the late 1970s, had a special local appeal as it played upon the Western Australian suspicion of the 'eastern-staters'. A book titled *Rumour in Orleans*, first published in 1969, details the consequences of this legend for six dress shops in the city of Orleans during the 1960s. The shops, all owned by Jews, became the target of anti-Semitic rumours that young women customers were being shanghaied into prostitution, yet the police had received no reports of such disappearances. Perhaps they went to Canberra?

The Kidnapped Daughter, told by a female high school student at a Western Australian school camp in 1987, is a variation on this theme. Just why anybody would be

shanghaied to our less-than-exciting national capital is a
mystery. Perhaps it is connected to Canberra's role as the
centre of the video porn distribution industry?

THE KIDNAPPED DAUGHTER

'My mother worked with this woman who told her a true story
about when she was in town on Saturday morning. Her
daughter needed to go to the toilet, so they went to one near
the Town Hall. There were a lot of people around at the time
and it wasn't far out of the way. Anyway, the girl entered the
toilet and her mother waited for her for about five minutes.

'She waited a while longer and started to get a bit worried,
so she went in to see what was taking so long. Just as she
walked in, another woman was walking out with the daughter,
who was looking sick. The woman with the girl said, "My
daughter is feeling sick — I'm taking her to hospital".

'Apparently the girl had been to the toilet and was at the
basin washing her hands, and this woman came up and
injected her with a needle and then tried to take her off
somewhere.'

A teacher that I know remembered this story being told to
her by her mother thirty years before, while another teacher
heard it recently. **The Kidnapped Daughter** is a variation of
the **Shanghaied to Canberra** story, and could crop up soon
featuring your local shopping mall!

ALL GONE!

A woman took her children to the Easter show, and one of them got lost. She searched frantically everywhere, but she had the other children with her, and they were slowing her down. A kind lady offered to mind the children for her while she searched for the lost one. After an hour of searching, she still couldn't find him, and decided to return to the kind lady to get her other children back. But the lady and the children had disappeared — the lady had taken them away. None of the children ever returned, so the woman lost her entire family on the one day.

This little chiller was sent to me by Pauline Bryant who heard it first in the early 1990s 'by a woman who had heard it from someone else'. Pauline gently suggested to the teller that it might just be an urban myth, but was told that it had happened for an absolute fact. Like the shopping centre abduction stories about ankle-slashers, this one trades on our fears, mostly unfounded, of crowds in public places. The disappearance of three children at the show would have excited national media interest, but I'll bet you can't recall the alleged incident either.

Closely related to these 'abduction at the shops' stories is the even nastier tale of **The Castrated Boy**.

THE CASTRATED BOY

A mother and her young son were out shopping and the boy needed to go to the toilet, so the mother quickly located the

public toilets and pushed the boy in through the door. She waited for him to come out and naturally became very worried when he didn't appear. So she alerted a male shopping centre employee, who went into the toilet to find out what had happened. The staff member discovered that the whole room was splattered with blood and the young boy was lying on the floor — castrated by a person or persons unknown.

Once again, the ordinary location of this gory story makes it especially appalling and memorable. The apparently motiveless nature of this incident echoes a frequently encountered concern with random acts of violence and cruelty. Events like the Hoddle Street massacre and the backpacker murders, covered in depth and detail by the press, provide real-life examples of random and chilling evil that encourage us to accept tales such as this.

[CHECKOUT CHECKS]

CAUGHT AT THE CHECKOUT

A girl walked into a supermarket and bought some groceries — a couple of things like bread and a carton of milk. At the checkout the woman in front of her turned around and said,

'Oh, my God, it's my daughter back from the dead. You're my daughter, aren't you?'

'No, I'm not your daughter,' the girl replied.

'You look so much like my daughter who died a couple of years ago. Would you do me a favour? When I leave and say "Goodbye", would you say "Goodbye, Mum", just for old times' sake?'

The girl agreed and did as she was asked when the woman left the store. Then, as the girl prepared to pay for her groceries, the checkout woman asked for $160.

'But I only bought a loaf of bread and milk!' she said.

'But your mum said you were going to pay for it.'

'No, that's not my mum,' said the girl.

'Yes it is. You said "Good-bye, Mum".'

As with most contemporary legends, the moral of this story is very clear. Don't do favours for strangers. If you do, you're likely to be sorry.

An extended version of this tale, collected by folklorist Dave Hults, has the girl running out of the shop and chasing down the scheming woman in the car park, just as she is getting into her car to make an escape. The girl grabs the woman by the leg and pulls it and pulls it. At this stage the listener wants to know what happens and asks the storyteller to continue. Having caught the listener, he or she smugly replies, 'She was pulling her leg, just like I'm pulling yours'. This 'catch-tale' version of the story is also told in America and, I expect, much further afield as well.

THE FROZEN CHOOK
AT THE CHECKOUT

A woman went into a supermarket to steal a chicken, but the only one she could lay her hands on was very large and deep frozen. The problem was that she hadn't brought a bag because she knew it would be searched. She was wearing a large hat, however, so she balanced the frozen chook underneath and made her way towards the checkout counter at the end of the store.

The checkout queue was very long and very slow. She waited and waited and waited, and eventually the cold of the chicken beneath her hat froze her brain. She collapsed and was rushed to hospital, but died of a chill on the brain.

The appeal of this simple little legend is its brevity and the clarity of the moral. It has been told in Sweden (where the shoplifter was male and the chook was a turkey), elsewhere in Scandinavia and in Germany since the early 1970s. By the time the story of the shoplifter with the chilled brains reached Britain in the late 1970s it featured a woman in the lead role. The story has been well-documented by folklorists in the United States, sometimes with the additional element of blood dripping from the chook or other meat hidden beneath the hat.

JUSTICE –
POETIC AND
OTHERWISE

THE MINISTER'S TELECARD

In October 2000 it was revealed that the federal Workplace Relations Minister, Mr Peter Reith, had run up a staggering $50,000 bill on his taxpayer-funded telecard account over the previous five years. The story that gradually came to light about these events is an example of an urban legend coming true, at least partly, a process known as 'ostension'.

While accounts varied, the basic facts of the telecard affair were that the minister had given his confidential ministerial telephone number and accompanying PIN to his son for use in an emergency. Somehow, the number came into the possession of various other individuals, and a huge bill was racked up in international calls.

The furore that erupted at these revelations naturally generated a witch hunt. A number of individuals and government departments were questioned as to how this had continued for five years, and why it had taken nine months for the minister to tell Parliament after he found out about it.

Mr Peter Reith had been caught up in a case of urban legend ostension. For many years, especially in the USA, a legend had circulated that the personal telephone credit card number of a celebrity — ranging from Johnny Carson to

Burt Reynolds — had been given out on TV for viewers to make use of. The number was distributed by word of mouth and in newsletters. Usually the fourteen digit number was a fake, although now and then it did turn out to be real, running up a huge debt on someone's (never the celebrity's) credit card account. In the legend, the allegedly wronged celebrity always managed to sue the telephone carrier for a large sum of money.

In the real life case of Mr Reith, the $50,000 telecard bill had to be paid back to the taxpayers by the minister himself. At this point, legend and reality parted company. But these parallels between fact and fantasy are an object lesson in the relationship between urban legends and reality. Perhaps truth is stranger than fiction, especially in politics.

A PLEASANT CHANGE

In June 1992 a young Sydney mother was changing her baby's nappy in the back seat of her car, while parked at a shopping mall. As she engaged in this messy but necessary task, a man walking by saw his opportunity, grabbed her bag and ran off into the crowd. The woman reported the theft to the shopping mall authorities, but did not seem to be at all distressed by her experience.

'You seem to be remarkably calm after an experience like that,' said the mall manager.

The young mother tucked her baby into the pram and smiled. 'The bag was full of dirty nappies,' she replied.

This mall story, in which the 'biter' is well and truly 'bit', contains another amusing piece of communal revenge.

Another version involves a urine specimen bottle. Unable to find the correct specimen jar, a woman who needed to provide the pathologist with a sample found an empty mini-whisky bottle in the house and used that instead. She was in such a hurry on her way to deliver the sample that she left the bottle on the car seat and forgot to lock the door. When she realised her error, she rushed back to the car to find that the bottle had been stolen by a thirsty thief. In some tellings of the tale the woman is found hunched over the wheel in convulsions. Fearing that she is having some kind of fit, a passer-by asked if she needed assistance. 'No thanks,' said the woman, raising her smiling face from the wheel, 'I simply can't stop laughing at what just happened to me.'

This yarn is related to stories reported elsewhere in the world, especially America, where it was first known in the early 1980s. In these similar stories a man (sometimes woman) has his bag stolen while walking his dog. When the thieves open the bag to examine their loot, they find it full of fresh doggy-do that the dog-walker had conscientiously scooped up.

It happened again in Des Moines, Iowa, in October 1999, according to *The Australian*'s 'Melba' column. Three teenagers grabbed a purse from the boot of Jo Ann Walker's car as she walked her dog in the park. Fido had answered the call of nature dogs always seem to get in public, grassy spaces, and Jo Ann had done the right thing. She had picked up the poo, wrapped it neatly, and deposited it temporarily in her purse, which she placed in the boot. According to 'Melba', as the miscreants ran off they had cheekily thanked Ms Walker. She was pleased to call back 'You're welcome!'

On the enthralling subject of excreta and crime, what can we make of the following?

ORDURE IN THE COURT

A man was being tried for a serious crime. Upon being found guilty, he immediately defecated into his hand and threw the fresh ordure at the judge. Unfortunately, the man's aim was poor and the turd hit the ceiling fan in the courtroom, spraying fresh poo all over the court, including the prisoner.

In early April 1998 I began hearing this odd little tale. I smiled indulgently at the teller and mentally did my folklorist's date check. Yep, a day or so after 1 April, just another April Fool prank.

About a week later, ABC radio news carried a remarkably similar item, with one or two variations. According to them, the incident occurred in India (explaining the ceiling fan in the court) and the guilty party had not achieved the remarkable feat of defecating on demand. Instead, his relatives had smuggled plastic bags full of fresh poo into court for his use, just in case.

Scenting a new legend here, I made discreet enquiries to friends and colleagues, quite a number of whom had heard versions of the story. Sometimes it happened in India, sometimes Indonesia, but wherever it was, it was somewhere 'foreign' — usually a reliable indicator of urban legendry at work.

I've heard no more of this intriguing anecdote, and have come across no mention of it in the usual sources. I have often wondered what sort of sentence the judge eventually pronounced on the poo-pelting prisoner, though.

7

BELIEVING IS SEEING:
SCAMS AND HOAXES

*G*RANNY ON THE ROOFRACK included a few examples of hoaxes and pranks that were by then firmly established in modern Australian folklore. These included the 'Nullarbor Nymph' of Western Australian fame (about which another book was recently published) and the 'Roaming Gnomes' phenomenon discussed in Chapter 5.

Since then, the growth of e-mail and the Internet has rapidly expanded the number and variety of hoaxes, pranks, false alarms and related misinformation let loose in the world. The anonymity of the net, the speed at which information can be transmitted, and the great numbers of people to whom messages can be simultaneously sent is proving the perfect vehicle for the transmission of all kinds of lore, including urban legends. Back in the mid–1990s, there were only a few cases of this e-lore. Now, in the 'noughties', most users of the net will have been the victims and perhaps unwitting perpetrators of hoaxes spread on the net. These include both tried and true favourites of the past, such as the Craig Shergold and similar fake appeals, and a quickly increasing repertoire of virus warnings, alarms and hoaxes. (More examples of this form of electronic delusion are included in the chapter titled 'Taking Care of Business').

So common have electronic legends and associated lore become that they are now developing their own folklore. Folklore about folklore, 'meta-folklore', usually in the form of a parody, is an increasingly encountered feature of modern urban lore. Readers who spend at least some of their working or leisure time on the net may well have encountered some of the 'real' urban legends included here, as well as the parody that I've called **Act Now!!!**

But as well as all this new-fangled nonsense, there is plenty of the old stuff still being purveyed in the traditional manner by word of mouth and the mass media. The section on 'cryptozoology' provides a few of many possible examples.

And finally, a cautionary tale that shows how frighteningly easy it is to be misled by the kind of false information, essentially modern superstitions or folk beliefs, on which urban legends are based.

[HOAXES]

HELL OF A WELL

Scientists deep drilling on the ocean bed recently tunnelled into hell. As the drill broke through the fourteen-kilometre level, tormented human screams were heard from below. The scientists fear they have unleashed the horrors of hell upon the earth.

It was December 1984 when the *Scientific American* magazine published a perfectly respectable article about the fascinating geological aspects of boring the world's deepest well. It seems that this may have been the basis of the well to hell story. An article purportedly translated from a Finnish publication was published in an American Christian broadcasting group's magazine titled *Praise the Lord,* and the story seems to have spread through evangelical Christian networks in the United States. Intrigued by this, the host of a Los Angeles talkback radio show tracked down the origins of the hellhole story to a Norwegian schoolteacher, who claimed to have fabricated it.

While all this sounds uncomfortably like an urban legend itself, Jan Brunvand provides the details in his 1993 book *The Baby Train*, and updates the tale in his 1999 publication *Too Good to Be True: The Colossal Book of Urban Legends*. Swedish folklorists began hearing about the well to hell around late 1990 to early 1991, and the tabloid newspaper *Weekly World News* ran the headline 'Satan Escapes from Hell' on 7 April 1992. The prince of darkness legged it via the hole in Alaska that year. The article was even accompanied by photographic evidence of an oil derrick ablaze, forming a huge cloud in the shape of Satan's head. Regrettably, it seems that *Weekly World News* journalists were unable to confirm Satan for an interview. No doubt, they are still hot on his trail.

As for Australia, Bill Scott came across a reference to a magazine article in which an archaeologist deep drilling on Cape York allegedly plumbed the infernal depths. I'd be interested to know if anyone else has come across this one which I feel an overwhelming urge to note, is a hell of a story.

DIHYDROGEN MONOXIDE (DHMO)

DHMO is an industrial solvent, coolant and fire retardant. It is a major contributor to the pollution caused by acid rain and inhalation of DHMO causes many deaths. Young children have died or been badly burned by DHMO. Despite these grave risks, government agencies continue to allow the use of DHMO in food preparation, as a food additive, in animal experimentation and waste management operations.

Nasty stuff. Dihydrogen Monoxide sounds a little bit like 'Dioxin', a real carcinogen. This is yet another Internet hoax that has been spreading around the world since the late 1990s. It generated considerable community concern and debate in many places until DHMO was revealed for what it was, hydric acid, H_2O — otherwise known as water.

As usual with such scares and urban legends in general, this one concentrates on a widespread concern, in this case with the health and environmental effects of industrial chemicals and processes. Like many such Internet hoaxes, this tale probably began life as a parody of real health alerts, but it did the job so well that many who received it believed it.

[REDEMPTIONS]

REDEMPTION BY POSTCARD

Contemporary rumours, legends and photocopy documents occasionally include what folklorists sometimes call 'redemption rumours' or 'redemption legends'. The most common theme for these stories is that an individual is seriously ill, sometimes dying, with some chronic disease (leukaemia, AIDS, kidney disease, etc). If people collect enough stamps, labels, postcards, soft drink can ring-pulls, teabag tags, potato chip packets, etc, and send them to a given address, money will be earned which will allow the afflicted individual to be sent somewhere (often Disneyland) for a last holiday. Alternatives are that the money will be used for a lifesaving operation, or to purchase an item of medical technology (perhaps a dialysis machine or pacemaker) to make life easier for the sufferer. Of course, there is almost always (see below) no such person and postal systems are needlessly burdened with tons of trivia.

The term 'redemption rumours', introduced by American folklorist Gary Alan Fine, refers both to the notion that these useless items can be redeemed for money (rather like the deposit on a returned soft drink bottle), and the emotional involvement of participants who feel they are redeeming themselves for their excessive dependence on consumer items that are unhealthy or bad for the environment. This explains why the objects specified for redemption are such irrelevant things as cigarette packets and plastic tags. Collecting these objects and putting them to good use is, Fine thinks, a way of salving our collective guilt.

You may prefer to think that the appeal of redemption rumours is that they offer an opportunity to do someone a good — even a lifesaving — turn for little outlay or effort. The fact that large numbers of people respond to such appeals, believing them to be valid, seems to indicate that 'the milk of human kindness' has not yet dried up. Redemption legends and rumours promote a positive aspect of human nature, unlike most of the other legends in this chapter.

Whatever the motivation behind them, the modern versions of redemption legends have been traced to the 1950s and, possibly, considerably earlier. And while there have been one or two American programs that did indeed redeem coupons for dialysis machines, redemption rumours are almost always just rumours. Probably the best-known of these was the 'Little Buddy' appeal. According to the story, Buddy was a young Scottish boy who was dying of either cancer or leukaemia or some other fatal disease. His ambition was to collect the largest number of postcards in order to secure an entry in the *Guinness Book of Records*. Would people help the little boy achieve his dying wish?

Would they! Transmitted by word of mouth, CB radio, print and photocopier, Little Buddy's appeal touched the world's heart in 1982. The postcards began arriving in Scotland from all over the world, including Australia. Pretty well anywhere in Scotland would do, it seems, although many went to Paisley. Despite disclaimers and debunkings, the rumour persisted and still reappears from time to time.

The 'Little Buddy Appeal' was, and is, a hoax, but a recent British case, that had extensive Australian repercussions, shows how rumour and reality can sometimes mesh. Craig Shergold, a ten-year-old boy from Surrey in England, was suffering from a brain tumour. Surgery had only been partly successful and he was undergoing chemotherapy. In September 1989, to cheer him up his family started an appeal to have a million get-well cards sent to Craig, a number that would get him into the *Guinness Book of Records*. Expatriate Aussie stars Kylie Minogue and Jason Donovan got involved, as did many other celebrities, and two months later Craig had achieved his aim. The appeal was halted by his family.

But the cards kept coming, and coming and coming, and the world's press picked up the story. A businessman in England started an international chain fax, appealing for get-well cards for Craig. The fax turned up all over Australia, as well as virtually everywhere else around the world with a facsimile machine system. The fax was also photocopied and placed on walls in public places around the world, including Australia. By Christmas 1989, even though the family had long since halted the appeal, the get-well cards were nudging the two million mark. By May 1990, Craig had received well over sixteen million get-well cards from all around the world, and they were still coming in. By Christmas that year some thirty-three million cards had been received and it was estimated that if these cards were all placed in stacks, they would make up ten Mount Everests.

As late as 1992, the story was being featured in newsletters and bulletins in Australia and this appeal for get-well cards has also made it onto the Internet, where it still pops up from time to time. In addition, from around mid-1992, the chain letters and faxes started asking for business cards instead of get-well cards. The Shergolds certainly didn't want *any* kind of card by then, but around 10,000 were arriving each day. Get-well cards are probably still driving Craig Shergold's local post office crazy.

In late 1994, reports were still coming in of Craig Shergold appeals being made in Canadian schools, and a further development of the appeal's spread was a kind of 'pyramid' chain letter. This worked by asking the recipient of the letter to send copies to ten more people, and to include the names of all the previous people in the chain. This technique rapidly multiplied the numbers of recipients and many such letters appeared in Australian offices and homes. I saw one of these posted on the wall of a hotel foyer near Mandurah, Western Australia, in 1989; the intention was obviously to inform as many guests as possible of the Craig Shergold Appeal.

Although the cards were not intended to assist Craig's medical condition, the resulting publicity brought about a real-life fairy tale ending. A book by Marian Shergold with Pamela Cockerill (*Craig Shergold: A Mother's Story*, condensed in the August 1994 edition of *Reader's Digest*) tells Craig's story and also reports that he has made a wonderful recovery. A wealthy American paid for Craig to have an operation in the United States, which has been successful. As Craig's mother said, 'It's like a fairy story'. She finished by asking that no more cards be sent — please!

Unfortunately, this one just will not go away. The legend has continued to proliferate through the Internet and e-mail throughout the 1990s and into 2001. Newspapers are still publishing notices stating that it was all a hoax, and that Craig does not want any more postcards, but they just keep on coming.

The Craig Shergold story is true, but the others are false; they are continuations of a long tradition of such beliefs and legends. Redemption rumours were around in the mid-nineteenth century and probably long before. The *Illustrated London News* of 13 May 1850 carried this item: 'Some time since there appeared in the public journals a statement to the effect that a certain young lady, under age, was to be placed in a convent by her father if she did not procure, before the 30th of April last, one million used postage stamps'. According to this article, the post office was overwhelmed with packages of used stamps sent by people around the country. The only thing that has changed since then is that the legend has become international rather than national, in accordance with the explosion of global communication.

But, please, no more postcards to Craig. Or Little Buddy, either. And no pop-tops . . .

REDEMPTION BY POP-TOP

The Internet plays an increasingly large role in the transmission of urban legends. Myths are rapidly spread around the world through this computer technology, and no matter how often or how apparently convincingly legends are discredited or debunked, we perversely persist in spreading them. The following exchange, which took place on the Internet late in 1994, reveals how easily modern legends are to spread, and how difficult it is to stop them.

The first message went like this:

'A few of us are collecting pop-tops from soda or beer cans for a cancer victim. For every milk jug full, she gets $100 off her chemotherapy. How about helping us to help someone else out by sending me your pop-tops? Please ... I'm not sure how this is going to work using this usegroup stuff, but I'll give it a try. Please spread the word and send your pop-tops to ...'

This well-intentioned appeal brought this reply:

'I'm sure you mean well, but ... this is an old urban legend. It's simply not true. Why would a hospital accept beer or soda pop-tops to pay for chemotherapy?

'One way you can tell this is an OLD urban legend is that pop-tops don't come off the way they used to several years ago. Also ... even if we suppose that the hospital recycles the pop-tops — why wouldn't they recycle the entire can? Wouldn't there be a lot more aluminium in a can?

'No ... unless [there is] PROOF that any hospital will do this, it's a terrible waste of time and energy.'

The original appealer responded:

'Yes, I do mean well, thank you. I am sorry that you feel I am wasting my time but I do not feel that way. (Even if I am wrong!) We have been collecting these for quite some time now and the girl who has cancer keeps taking them. I hardly feel she would be wasting her time and ours if she didn't need them.

'She was also told that the pop-tops are 100 per cent aluminium, whereas the cans are not. That is why they only want the tops.

'A friend of mine (who is the friend of the girl who has cancer) will be forwarding the name of the hospital to me so you can verify it. No-one wants anyone to waste their time helping someone else if it really won't work.

'Thanks for your concern ... As soon as I get the name and address of the hospital, I'll be more than happy to send it to you.'

The hospital's name and address have not yet appeared on the Internet. But since this early example of Internet transmission of urban legends, redemption legends have been running hot, hot, hot on the web, as the e-mail reproduced below demonstrates only too well.

SLOW DANCE

Have you ever watched kids on a merry-go-round,
Or listened to the rain slapping on the ground?
Ever followed a butterfly's erratic flight,
Or gazed at the sun into the fading light?

You'd better slow down,
Don't dance so fast,
Time is short,
The music won't last.

Do you run through each day on the fly
When you ask 'How are you?' do you hear the reply?

When the day is done, do you lie in your bed,
With the next hundred chores running through your head?

You'd better slow down,
Don't dance so fast,
Time is short,
The music won't last.

Ever told your child 'We'll do it tomorrow',
And in your haste, not seen his sorrow?
Ever lost touch, let a good friendship die,
'Cause you never had time to call and say 'Hi'?

You'd better slow down,
Don't dance so fast,
Time is short,
The music won't last.

When you run so fast to get somewhere,
You miss half the fun of getting there.
When you worry and hurry through your day,
It is like an unopened gift . . . thrown away.

Life is not a race.
Do take it slower,
Hear the music,
Before the song is over.

PLEASE FORWARD THIS TO HELP A LITTLE GIRL.

According to the affecting letter that accompanies this
poetic plea, it is the last wish of an unnamed little girl dying
of cancer 'to send a chain letter telling everyone to live their

life to the fullest, since she never will. She'll never make it to prom, graduate to high school, or get married and have a family of her own. By sending this message to as many people as possible, you can give her and her family a little hope, because The American Cancer Society will donate three cents per name to her treatment and recovery plan. One guy sent this to five hundred people!!!!'

Sound familiar? Unfortunately, there is no such little girl and the American Cancer Society does not donate three cents per e-mail. How could the society possibly *know* how many e-mails had been sent? (Another version of this story includes the line 'All forwarded e-mails are tracked to obtain the total count', an attempt to plug the gaping hole in the credibility of this 'appeal'.)

Who is this little girl? In some versions she is named as a 'Jessica Myadek', but she doesn't exist either. And where is she? If she is dying, why is there a 'recovery plan' for her? And there are the multiple exclamation marks again, the sure sign of the hoaxer's attempts to generate a false suggestion of urgency and importance.

Like most of the redemption hoaxes, this one attempts to cloud the receiver's judgement by targeting their emotions. By the time you get halfway through reading the e-mail, you're ready to mortgage the house for the poor little mite. Don't do it. And don't send the message on, no matter how moved you are. The best way to help cancer sufferers is to donate to the appropriate organisations.

The above version of 'Slow Dance', received in September 1999, was prefaced by three and a half pages of e-mail addresses to which the same message had been sent. A little less than a year earlier, I had received the same e-mail from another source that was part of a Christmas greetings message, prefaced with barely half a page of e-mail addresses. This highlights the growth of electronic communication over the period and also the rapidity with which such messages can be distributed to dozens, hundreds, even thousands of individuals almost instantaneously. Even if only a fraction of those who receive such messages forward them through their own mail lists, it's not hard to see why urban legends and associated forms of modern mythology are on the increase.

E-mail also provides the perfect communications network for transmitting panic and misinformation. As with **Blue Star Acid** and other hoax scares, these are usually passed on by genuinely concerned people who have been taken in by a prankster. Like the Craig Shergold and Little Buddy legends, this one has taken in a very great number of people — certainly millions, perhaps tens of millions. The American Cancer Society has been forced to place a debunking statement about it on their website at: www.cancer.org/letter.html.

[ALARMS]

BURGLARY ALERT

Please pass this on, as this sort of thing has been happening in Melbourne and is moving to Sydney.

There is a big scam going on where a person calls and says that they are doing a computer survey from a company. The company name that they give is usually a big well-known

software company, and they usually say that they are doing the survey because they want to give out free software. They want to know what would be a good time for someone to come from their company and install the software on your PC. They also ask questions about income, etc. During their questioning they (unknowingly to you) find out what time you're usually home, what kind of computer equipment you have and all sorts of other valuable information.

At a company where a friend of mine works, a co-worker of his received one of these calls, and he was robbed the very next day (of course, when he was not home). I received a similar call yesterday afternoon. Fortunately, I knew about this ahead of time, and didn't provide them with any information. I want to make you all aware of the situation and the potential danger involved in giving out any information like this over the phone. The people sound very genuine, and very few people are going to question receiving free software. I would advise you, however, to tell the people that if they have your phone number, they should have your address, and they can mail you any free software they might be offering. If you have a home computer set-up, you should be familiar with installing your own software. You may even want to tell them you don't have a home computer. Whatever you're comfortable with.

Please don't give out any information that you may regret later. Pass this information along to friends and family members, as well. The fewer people they are able to burgle, the better.

I have removed the name of the genuinely concerned citizen who forwarded this to 'everyone' in February 1997 — many of whom probably did the same.

What we have here is an update of an old story about the 'cold-calling' giveaway offer where someone calls and finds out details of your domestic routine with the aim of robbing you while you are out. It is certainly one way that criminals operate. The detail of 'the co-worker of a friend of mine', though, puts this story straight into the FOAF category, although the writer also claims to have been approached himself.

This is perhaps a case of urban legendry fulfilling a useful purpose. The events described may or may not have happened. Nevertheless, such things are known to occur, and it does no harm to remind people to be careful when giving personal information to unknown individuals offering free gifts.

There seems to be an increasing number of such 'alarms' on the Internet, including messages that alert single women to the dangers of staying in hotels and provide common-sense advice about how to protect themselves.

The situations described in these messages are typical of urban legends and they also have the intention of alerting the receiver to a perceived danger. The difference between these probably genuine alarms and those that simply seek to frighten you are that these communications have a more quietly serious tone, devoid of multiple exclamation marks and logical inconsistencies, unlike the example elsewhere in this chapter titled **It Takes Guts to Say 'Jesus'**.

TRICK OR TREAT?

The Halloween custom of 'trick-or-treating', which has long been popular in America, has spread to many parts of Australia in recent years. Although Halloween (31 October, All Hallows' Eve, and 1 November, All Hallows' Day) has a long tradition in Britain and is a Christianisation of the Celtic festival of Samhain that marked the end of an agricultural year and the transition to the next, the form in which it has come to Australia is mainly from the United States.

In that country the festival involves the practice of 'trick-or-treat', in which children, dressed up as witches, ghouls or ghosts, knock at neighbours' doors and ask 'Trick or treat?' The threat in this statement is that if the kids are not given lollies or other suitable bribes they will do something terrible to the neighbour's mailbox, fence, front yard, rubbish bin or cat.

This custom is now rather out of hand in the United States, and neighbours are no longer prepared to tolerate the little ghouls from down the street doing increasingly serious damage to their property on All Hallows' Eve. It is widely rumoured that some victims have struck back by giving the kids poisoned lollies, or they have secreted powdered glass, broken razor blades and other nasty things in the 'treats'. There may be a few documented cases of such occurrences, but the general belief has grown that this is a common event, with stories of children's goodies being X-rayed just in case, and of children becoming seriously ill and even dying from the results of such adult evil.

These rumours have now reached Australia, where they've spread with a fervour that seems at odds with the relatively insignificant practice of trick-or-treating. No doubt horrific stories are in the interests of those who do not wish to see 'pagan' customs catch on here, as well as parents made anxious by the stories of American cruelties.

As Halloween trick-or-treating has become firmly established in Australia, despite the unhappiness of the church and many parents, I've left this item in much as it was in *Great Australian Urban Myths*. It can be usefully compared with the more recent development of the upturned syringes in the playground under the title **The Used Syringes**.

BLUE STAR ACID

NOTICE FOR PARENTS OF SCHOOL-AGE CHILDREN
'A form of tattoo called "Blue Star" is being sold to school children. It is a sheet of white paper containing a blue star, the size of a pencil eraser. Each star is soaked in LSD and can be removed and placed in the mouth. The LSD can be absorbed through the skin by handling the paper.

'There are also brightly coloured tabs resembling postage stamps that have pictures of Superman, butterflies, clowns, Mickey Mouse and other Disney characters on them. These are packed in a red cardboard box wrapped in foil. This is a new way of selling acid by appealing to young children. A young child could happen on these and have a fatal "trip". Small children could be given a free "tattoo" by other children who want to have some fun, or by others cultivating new customers.

'A red stamp called "Red Pyramid" is also being distributed, along with "Micro Dot" which comes in various colours. Yet another kind, "Window Pane", has a grid that can be cut out. These are all laced with drugs. If sighted, do not handle them. These drugs are known to react very quickly and some are laced with strychnine. The symptoms are hallucination, severe vomiting, uncontrollable laughter, mood changes and change in body temperature. The victims should go to hospital and notify police as soon as possible.'

In Sydney's populous western suburbs, in early 1990, a drug-scare legend took hold and spread rapidly. This legend was circulated not only by word of mouth and the media, but also by means of a crudely typed and photocopied flyer or handbill, the text of which is reproduced above. The flyer was posted in public places — shopping malls, banks, community centres — and explicitly warned of LSD-soaked transfers being sold to school children. This one was found in the Commonwealth Bank at Penrith in April 1990.

Despite its obviously home-made character, the flyer managed to give the impression that it was some sort of official warning. The police were forced to point out that the document was not authorised by themselves or by drug referral centres, but they were bombarded with calls from concerned parents and school principals around Penrith, and from as far away as Parramatta. The police, informed these callers that they had no knowledge of such a drug being available in the area.

The scare hit Perth at the same time and was broadcast as a true story on the popular 'Howard Sattler Show' (6PR) on 4 April. The reaction here was much the same as that in Sydney and the many other places around the world where this legend arose. The police in Britain had to make similar public pronouncements to those of their Penrith counterparts when the same scare hit that country in 1993.

By late 1995 the LSD tattoo had reached the north-west of Western Australia. The *North-West Telegraph* of 6 December 1995, reported that a copy of the flyer had been forwarded to local MLC, Tom Helm. The copy that came to Helm was derived from one of the American sources, as it purported to come from Danbury Hospital (see below). The north-westerners, a no-nonsense lot, were not sure if the warning was authentic and sensibly tried to validate it. They could not, but in case it was for real decided to take no chances and used it as part of their local drug awareness program. Mr Helm indicated his intention of asking a question about the matter in Parliament.

But there is no such thing as 'Blue Star Acid', or any similar substance being peddled to the children of the world. These allegations have been investigated again and again by police, medical authorities, journalists, folklorists and others. While LSD in blotting paper form is often decorated with artwork, including the occasional cartoon character, there is no evidence that such products are being peddled to children. Jan Brunvand's 1989 book *Curses! Broiled Again* (pp.55–64) includes details of extensive, and almost totally fruitless police investigations of this hoax up to the late 1980s. He interviewed William Hopkins, director of the Bureau of Research for the State of New York Division of Substance Abuse Services. Hopkins's department carried out a survey of 450 law enforcement agencies in early 1988 to discover if there was 'an impending disaster' of Blue Star Acid peddling. The results showed a statistically insignificant occurrence of LSD carrying a blue star or cartoon character for the period of 1985–1987. The official report stated that the flyers and letters about Blue Star Acid were 'a hoax and should be treated as such.'

The findings of the now many investigations like this have been widely and unequivocally published by hospitals, writers and the United States Drug Enforcement Administration. In these refutations it is variously pointed out that, even if Blue Star Acid or its equivalent did exist, the likelihood of a child absorbing sufficient LSD through his or her fingers to experience a 'trip' is almost non-existent. Numerous other medical, logical, legal and investigative points are made, as in the report first issued by the DEA in 1992 and re-issued in June 1996. This pointed out the nature of the hoax and also confirmed that no evidence of a child being harmed by an 'LSD-laden tattoo' had been found.

A number of hospitals have been at the centre of this rumour and, as a result, have been driven to publicly refute the stories. On 29 September 1993, the Danbury Hospital,

Connecticut, issued a press release in response to a flyer about Blue Star Acid printed on the hospital's own letterhead. The hospital stated clearly that it had no involvement with the hoax memo.

Other hospitals have issued even stronger refutations. The Cincinnati Drug and Poison Information Center issued an explicit statement in late 1993 pointing out that LSD cannot be absorbed through intact skin and that the Blue Star Acid and related scares were 'folklore'.

All these refutations have been to little or no avail. The Blue Star – Mickey Mouse – Bart Simpson sticker – tattoo – transfer panic not only fails to go away, it seems to be getting stronger. Despite authoritative denial and professional investigation, large numbers of individuals around the world continue to believe in this story, prolonging the near-global moral panic by aggressively distributing the hoax warnings at every possible opportunity and venue, now including the Internet. Genuinely concerned persons are willing to spuriously use the official letterhead, logos and other trappings of institutions like hospitals and corporations in order to give the story credibility.

Fear and ignorance about drugs and drug abuse is one of the great social paranoias of the late twentieth and early twenty-first century. Like the AIDS pandemic and the Satanic Ritual Abuse scare, such moral panics obsessively focus our insecurities onto a single, simple explanation. These 'explanations', like the rumours that fill the vacuum of hard information in wartime, are ways in which people desperately seek to 'make sense' of an aspect of life that they do not understand and over which they have no control. At least printing and distributing flyers and sending e-mail messages to Internet groups concerned with children is *something* positive and constructive. The tragedy is that these actions would be useful if they were not in the service of a delusion. In the meantime, the diversion of resources gives the real drug dealers of the world an undeserved break.

As with many other contemporary legends, this one seems to have started in the United States of America, where it was reported in the early 1980s. Since then the scare has turned up either as Blue Star Acid, the Mickey Mouse version or the more recent Bart Simpson rendition around the world. A similar story surfaced in Dusseldorf, Cologne and Hamburg, in Germany, and elsewhere in Europe in 1989. In 1990 the legend surfaced again and was reported in Canada.

Usually the flyer is spread by genuinely concerned people, as the documentation of the scare that Dan Gross provided on his 'Blue Star Acid' website indicates. A selection of Gross's extensive collection shows that the flyer is internationally distributed, turning up in Newfoundland in 1990; Spain and the US Embassy in Lima, Peru, in 1988; South Africa in 1989 and again in 1996; Italy in 1996; and all over the United States. It has also been distributed to schools (Muhlenberg College Faculty and Staff Parents, 5 February 1989; a Texas elementary school in March 1996) and corporate or government bureaucracies (March 1997 at DuPont Chemicals in Victoria, Texas; NASA Langley Research Center in May 1996; and IBM in January 1994), to name only some.

The link between such relatively limited bureaucratic distributions and injection of the scare into the larger population through the mass media is also usefully highlighted in Gross's chronology. He picks up the Du Pont Chemical flyer being printed, almost verbatim, in the March 1997 edition of a local newspaper in Yorktown, Texas. This is one of the important ways that urban legends and other forms of misinformation, such as rumour, are spread. They move quickly around the private or restricted forums of interest groups or work groups, thus gaining a spurious aura of authority — 'everyone is talking about it'. This then allows them to be picked up by representatives of the more formal communications industries, many of whom obviously do not check the sources of their information. The newspapers or magazines reprint the warning, as a public service, but community panic ensues.

The flyer was transmitted by mail, fax, hand, on the walls and notice boards of public and private buildings, as in the Penrith case. Especially prominent as sources of dissemination are small-scale newsletters and special interest publications such as the 'Mosquito Squadron' newsletter, Winter 1995, *The Village Voice* (a community association newsletter) in June 1996, and in Lansing (New York) *Central School District Bulletin*, 'A Warning To Parents: An Appeal To The Young.'

From 1996 the Internet and e-mail begin to take over as the main means of dissemination, with home schooling, parental and family oriented newsgroups being favourite targets. From this point onwards, individuals, and the odd parodist, took advantage of the new technology to spread the word. Unfortunately, the word was and is wrong, and has been shown to be on many occasions. But this has not stopped the progress of Blue Star Acid through cyberspace. It is posted in all sorts of places — sites and user groups that attract parents and teachers are the favourites.

Those who post it are clearly worried by the flyer. They make comments like 'This may not be in your area yet!!!!! But I am passing it along as an awareness process' (January 1996) and 'The content is so important that I want to post it here'. In February 1996, the usenet newsgroup alt.child-support received the warning with the sender's comment: 'I do not know the source or if it is true but it sounds real enough to me'. This last note goes to the nub of the problem. Even though people do not necessarily believe the flyer, they think that it just might be true, so they pass it on. Sometimes senders will admit that they have not validated the information but are passing it on anyway, as in an e-mail to ParcPlace-Digitalk in May of 1996: 'I have not personally substantiated it, but the topic is too important to ignore out of hand'.

This is the merest skimming of the surface of the transmission of the Blue Star Acid scare around the world. The same process is going on in hundreds, if not thousands, of informal and formal communication networks across the globe, aided and abetted by the Internet and e-mail. The wonder then, is not that we occasionally experience a new burst of this scare, as Perth did in late 1998, but that it is not even more prevalent.

Whatever the origins of this excessively tenacious tale, you can be assured that extensive research by police and other officials throughout America has conclusively shown this legend, in all its variations, is untrue. Children are not being peddled the drugs described in the photocopied notice; nor are there in existence any postage stamps soaked in LSD. However, the truth seems unlikely to stop this story which, like many legends, trades on our fear of contaminated 'edibles' and concern for the safety of children.

The real worry is that this long-lasting, widespread and alarming hoax has now been around so long, it may have actually created a demand from drug users for such a product that dope peddlers will be only too willing to satisfy. The no-doubt right-minded individuals who circulate this hoax may be creating the very situation that they are warning against. Another potential example of ostension, an urban legend coming true.

VIRUSES AND WORMS

IT TAKES GUTS TO SAY 'JESUS'

Subject: Fw: WARNING
Sent: 8/4/99 10:21 pm
Received: 12/4/99 12.26 am
WARNING
If you receive an email titled 'It Takes Guts to Say Jesus' DO
NOT OPEN IT. It will erase everything on your hard drive. This
information was announced yesterday morning from IBM; AOL
[America Online] states that this is a very dangerous virus,
much worse than 'Melissa', and that there is NO remedy for it
this time.

Some very sick individual has succeeded in using the re-
format function from Norton Utilities, causing it to completely
erase all documents on the hard drive. It has been designed to
work with Netscape Navigator and Microsoft Internet Explorer.
It destroys Macintosh and IBM compatible computers. This is a
new, very malicious virus and not many people know about it.

Pass this warning along to EVERYONE in your address book
and please share it with all our online friends ASAP so that
this threat may be stopped. Please practice cautionary
measures and tell anyone that may have access to your
computer. Forward this warning to everyone that might access
the Internet.

This message appeared in my inbox one day in April 1999. The date is significant, as this e-mail probably began life in the United Kingdom as an April Fools' Day prank — yet another modern electronic extension of an old folk custom.

The problem with virus warnings and most other e-mail communications, is that it is hard to tell the genuine from the spurious. One danger sign is the tone of panic that these messages almost always adopt. A second red light is that like a chain letter or pyramid-selling scam, you are always urged, usually more than once, to pass the warning on to anyone and everyone. Other danger signs are the excessive use of CAPITALS and 'scare quotes'. And hoaxes like these almost always invoke a well-known disaster to worry you even more — the example above refers to the infamous Melissa virus that wreaked havoc on the computer world in 1999.

As many of these features are pretty commonly encountered in e-mail speak, how is a poor recipient to know if he or she is being hoaxed or not? The first thing to do is to check with your local web-controller, or whoever looks after your system. They may be as much in the dark as you, so point your browser to a website for virus hoaxes.

ELECTRONIC WORMS

According to the International Computer Security Association virus attacks by e-mail have increased rapidly since 1996. In 1999 they recorded an increase of 56 per cent over the previous year, which had recorded a 32 per cent increase over attacks in 1997. Even more worrying for businesses and all computer users is the fact that an increasing proportion of these attacks are not old-fashioned viruses, but what the industry call 'worms'. Unlike viruses, worms do not need human help in the form of e-mail messages to replicate themselves. They can be spread from just one infected file on a single machine, and from there can bore through entire systems. The anti-virus software organisation Symantec estimates that over the next decade worms will overtake viruses as the main form of attack on computer systems.

While all this sounds rather like the frenzy generated by certain sections of the computer industry in relation to the Millennium Bug, there is no doubt that viruses and worms can, and have caused enormous costly damage to computer systems and the businesses that use them. One of the most notorious of these was the 1999 'Melissa virus', which was apparently a worm. Others have included LoveLetter, ILOVEYOU and Explore-Zip. In the second half of 2000 the major threats were said to be the Wscript.kakWorm and the Pretty-Park.Worm.

With such a variety of electronic menaces crawling through cyberspace, it is not surprising that anxiety levels in the net community have been raised in the same way as tensions can arise in the real world. This situation replicates the ideal conditions for the creation and spread of virus and worm hoaxes.

The ease with which the Internet can fool even highly intelligent people, and the cell-multiplication-like speed at which it can infect extremely large numbers of 'hosts' is demonstrated by what should be a well-known computer virus hoax. Someone places the hoax scare into the e-mail system, safe in the knowledge that someone, somewhere in some genuine organisation will swallow it and pass it on.

A couple of popular examples of this are the 'Join the Crew' and 'Penpal Greetings' hoax. The message, received by staff at Curtin University on 14 August 1997, went like this: 'If you receive an e-mail message titled "Join the Crew" or "Penpal Greetings", do not open it, as they are viruses that will destroy all your computer files, and eat your hard drive'. In tones of fear and panic, the receiver was urged to pass this warning on to as many others as possible: 'Forward this ASAP to every single person you know!!!!!!!!!'

The university's computer watchdog distributed a message debunking the host — far too late, of course, as it had already been sent on its many ways. A pity someone didn't check first.

At the time of writing, no worm hoaxes have yet come my way. Hopefully none have come your way, either. But history suggests it is just a matter of time before they wriggle into your virtual life. In the meantime, here's a well-constructed parody of e-mail chain letters.

ACT NOW!!!

The dawn of the electronic communication age has made redemption rumours so widespread and numerous, that they are now the subject of folk parodies distributed via the Internet. Folklorists, always quick to develop their own in-group lore, have a jargon name for this phenomenon called 'meta-folklore' — folklore about folklore. A familiar example of this is the parody chain letter. The chain letter that promises you great wealth if you send it on, and threatens dire consequences if you don't, has been around for at least a century. It has become so familiar that, like an increasing number of urban legends, it has developed its own meta-folklore.

Two examples of parody chain letters are included in my 1997 book *The Bare Fax*, namely the 'Chain Letter for Women' and 'The Fertilizer Club'. Since then, e-mail has encouraged the proliferation of other clever examples. One of these is the fake warning about the 'Gullibility Virus' said to be spreading over the Internet.

Warning, Caution, Danger, and Beware!
Gullibility Virus Spreading over the Internet!

Washington, D.C. — The Institute for the Investigation of Irregular Internet Phenomena announced today that many Internet users are becoming infected by a new virus that causes them to believe without question every groundless story, legend and dire warning that shows up in their inbox or on their browser. The Gullibility Virus, as it is called, apparently makes people believe and forward copies of silly hoaxes relating to cookie recipes, e-mail viruses, taxes on modems, and get-rich-quick schemes.

'These are not just readers of tabloids or people who buy lottery tickets based on fortune cookie numbers,' a spokesman said. 'Most are otherwise normal people, who would laugh at the same stories if told to them by a stranger on a street corner.' However, once these same people become infected with the Gullibility Virus, they believe anything they read on the Internet.

'My immunity to tall tales and bizarre claims is all gone,' reported one weeping victim. 'I believe every warning message and sick child story my friends forward to me, even though most of the messages are anonymous.' Another victim, now in remission, added, 'When I first heard about Good Times [a

reference to a "genuine" Internet hoax], I just accepted it without question. After all, there were dozens of other recipients on the mail header, so I thought the virus must be true.' It was a long time, the victim said, before she could stand up at a Hoaxees Anonymous meeting and state, 'My name is Jane, and I've been hoaxed.' Now, however, she is spreading the word. 'Challenge and check whatever you read,' she says.

Internet users are urged to examine themselves for symptoms of the virus, which include the following:

- The willingness to believe improbable stories without thinking
- The urge to forward multiple copies of such stories to others
- A lack of desire to take three minutes to check to see if a story is true

T.C. is an example of someone recently infected. He told one reporter, 'I read on the Net that the major ingredient in almost all shampoos makes your hair fall out, so I've stopped using shampoos.' When told about the Gullibility Virus, T.C. said he would stop reading his e-mails, so that he would not become infected.

Anyone with symptoms like these is urged to seek help immediately. Experts recommended that at the first feelings of gullibility, Internet users should rush to their favourite search engine and look up the item tempting them to thoughtless credence. Most hoaxes, legends and tall tales have been widely discussed and exposed by the Internet community.

This message is so important, we're sending it anonymously! Forward it to all your friends right away! Don't think about it! This is not a chain letter! This story is true! Don't check it out! This story is so timely, there is no data on it! This story is so important, we're using lots of exclamation points! Lots!! For every message you forward to some unsuspecting person, the

Home for the Hopelessly Gullible will donate ten cents to itself. (If you wonder how the Home will know you are forwarding these messages all over creation, you're obviously thinking too much.)
ACT NOW! DON'T DELAY! LIMITED TIME ONLY!
NOT SOLD IN ANY STORE!

Authored by an anonymous professional writer, probably a journalist, this amusing parody of the Internet alarm highlights the various danger signs that are a feature of this form of e-lore.

There are a good number of sites on the World Wide Web that provide information about viruses, bugs and hoaxes, including the following:

www.lostparadise.com/hoaxes.html

www.kumite.com/myths/myths/

www.wvmccd.cc.ca.us/wvc/oth/erodrigues/hoax/

Many hoax and virus sites are also involved in urban legend monitoring.

[CRYPTOZOOLOGY]

'ABC'S

For cryptozoology read 'weird animals and things'. For 'ABC's read 'Alien Big Cats' — not alien in the sense of coming from outer space (plenty of myths there, of course), but alien in the sense of not belonging to a particular place. This is what cryptozoologists, the people who study this sort of thing, call the mysterious animals that have long populated the Australian imagination.

To some extent it is misleading to place this section in a chapter on hoaxes and scams. There is certainly plenty of scope for these activities in the realm of cryptozoology, but there are also many people who genuinely believe in the existence of mysterious panthers, leopards, tigers and the like and spend a great deal of time and money pursuing their beliefs. These beliefs may also include such fabulous creatures as yowies and bunyips.

In what is probably the most extended folkloric study of weird animals undertaken to date in Australia, Bill Scott notes 'There is certainly a very strong folk belief in this country of the existence of such an animal, which is usually described by witnesses as a panther or a big cat' (*Pelicans and Chihuahuas*, p.27). Scott goes on to identify a number of these beasties recovered from his own fieldwork and from various secondary sources. These include the Emmaville Panther (NSW), the Kangaroo Valley Panther (NSW), the Waterford Panther (QLD), the Dromana Mountain Lion (Vic), the Marulan Tiger (NSW), and the Guyra Cat (NSW). To these could be added the Tasmanian Tiger and the Nannup Tiger (WA) and the Kyneton Cat (Vic), among many other ABCs. There are cougars around Townsville, Mount Spec and even Charters Towers. In fact, just about anywhere that Europeans have occupied this continent you can find local ABC legends.

What most of the Australian sightings of such ABCs have in common are descriptions of animals that resemble 'big cats' and, often venerable explanations of how such alien creatures came to be prowling the Australian bush. One favoured explanation is that a pair of panthers (or cougars, or mountain lions) were brought here as mascots for US troops during World War II. After the war, the pair was set loose into the bush and nature took its course. No-one has yet come up with any documentation of such animals or their cavalier release into our wildlife. In fact, many of the accounts of such creatures long predate the 1942–45 period.

Other common factors in mystery cat lore include the almost obligatory photograph or, in recent years, video footage, that provides irrefutable evidence of the existence of such beasts. When — and if — these are produced, they always turn out to be murky snaps taken in semi-darkness that could be anything from a big ginger tom to a dog. The ambivalence of mysterious beast photographs is matched only by those of flying saucers.

But what about the footprints? Ah yes, another important element of big cat lore are the outsized, backward-pointing or otherwise odd tracks supposedly left by the beasts. Plaster casts are invariably made of these prints for examination by experts, whose job it is to vindicate the beliefs of those who found the tracks. In such cases, the experts findings are rarely heard.

Naturally, farmers who find their stock savaged to death want to know what did it so they can go out and kill it. But while reports of such events, in some cases, go well back into the nineteenth century, no-one has ever produced an authenticated mysterious cat, tiger or other beast — alive or dead. Busselton (WA) farmers suffered a series of unexplained sheep losses over 1997–98. They believed the deaths and disappearances to be the work of wild cougars. The regulation plaster casts of the suspected animal's prints were made and given to Perth Zoo for inspection. Their verdict? Carnivore keeper Trueman Faulkner was 'unable to determine what had left the print, but said it was not large enough to be a cougar', according to the *Sunday Times* of 7 March 1999. He was further quoted as saying 'The claws have the characteristics of a cat ... But I would not like to put my money on it being a big cat, it could even be a large dog'.

Similar conclusions have been reached by other experts who have examined such evidence. In the mid–1970s a Deakin University study was conducted into reports of pumas in the Grampians. As reported in *The Weekend Australian* of 12–13 August 2000, environmental science students collected plaster casts of the footprints, fur, bone, fibre and even some puma poo. These were sent to puma specialists in Colorado. The findings of the specialists were carefully worded, but said the specimens were consistent with pumas. 'It was tantalising but not conclusive,' said Professor John Henry, the academic in charge of the investigation. Henry decided to look for more evidence. He had heard the story that the US Airforce had released big cats into the Grampians during World War II. So he tracked down six ex-members and put it to them in writing. Some of the servicemen recalled hearing stories about such things but were reluctant to go further. The Deakin team's report, which has never been published, was unable to prove the existence of pumas in the Grampians but noted evidence of 'large carnivores other than wild dogs'.

The *Australian* article had been sparked by a reported sighting and video footage of an ABC in the area and the subsequent television screening of this 'evidence'. As the article noted, 'the new video footage has failed to convince officials in Victoria's Department of Natural Resources, who thought the most likely explanation for the ABC on the video was 'a feral cat'. A spokesman said: 'We will remain sceptical about the exotic cat theory until field evidence comes along, rather than hearsay of sightings'.

BUNYIPS, YOWIES AND YARAMAS

Even more intriguing than ABCs are stories of bunyips and yowies. These are definitely 'our' legends, rural if not urban. Bunyips live in billabongs and other water bodies, waiting to drag unwary passers-by into the depths. They are based upon indigenous beliefs about water spirits and, having been anglicised for a couple of centuries, now have a good deal in common with similar beings from other traditions, including the English Ginny (Jenny) Greenteeth, among other such creatures that populate the world's folk traditions.

In his book *Bunyips and Bigfoots: In Search of Australia's Mystery Animals*, Malcolm Smith, cryptozoologist — and a real zoologist to boot — provides an excellent and well-documented overview of our intriguing and weird animals. Smith reviews beast reports from around the country and from New Zealand. He covers bunyips and he does a good line in sea serpents, too. He also tracks down the local version of 'bigfoot', the ape-like yowie.

The yowie is derived from Aboriginal beliefs about a fierce, hairy male or female creature. The earliest mention of it seems to be 1835, though no-one claimed to have seen one until 1871. Since then there have been many reported sightings, though the term 'yowie' does not appear to have come into general use until 1975. I certainly don't recall hearing the word before the 1980s. Be that as it may, on 8 September 2000, Australian Associated Press carried reports of a bushwalker who had footage of a large creature he believed could be a yowie. As reported in the *West Australian* newspaper of 9 September, the bushwalker filmed a mystery creature in Canberra's Brindabella Ranges, a favourite yowie lair. The bushwalker was quoted in the report as saying 'I was filming what I thought was a large kangaroo in a gully, when I realised it was far too big to be a roo'. Perhaps it was a kangaroo wearing a tourist's overcoat?

Queensland writer and folklore collector Rosemary Opala writes of the little-known yarama that lurks up her way. Inhabiting tropical coastal forests they are 'diabolical spirits, four feet tall with huge heads, mouths, throats and bellies; are covered with scaly green and red skin and have cup-shaped suckers for fingers and toes'. The 'yuk factor' is ringing the bell at the top of the scale here. The yaramas like to perch in fig trees and pounce on passing humans, fastening their suckers and draining the victim's blood, then they eat what's left.

According to legend, should the victim be tough enough to survive and, Jonah-like, be regurgitated, the yarama would get revenge by drinking the community's water supply. And, just in case you thought the worst was over, the victim always turns into a yarama. Our very own indigenous vampire myth.

The alligators are still in the sewers, too.

ALLIGATORS IN THE SEWERS

A man went on holiday to an exotic location where alligators live, and was so taken with the antics of the reptiles that he took a couple of baby alligators back to his apartment. As the creatures grew, the holiday-maker decided they weren't so attractive and unceremoniously flushed them down the toilet. The alligators survived and bred down in the sewer system which was consequently inhabited by hordes of reptiles, who snapped off the odd sewerman. The existence of these subterranean beasts was, not surprisingly, kept a secret by city officials, who feared a mass panic if the fact became known.

As numerous people have pointed out, this popular yarn is not new — versions involving wild hogs in the London sewers were around in nineteenth-century England. An American researcher found a 1935 newspaper report of an alligator in a New York sewer, and there is some documented evidence, surveyed in Jan Brunvand's *The Vanishing Hitchhiker,* of the existence of sewer reptiles in New York in the 1930s. Whatever the truth of the tale, it has been used a number of times by fiction writers, including the great modern American novelist Thomas Pynchon.

Then there are the flesh-eating piranhas discovered in the storm drains of Singapore, late in 1991. According to the *West Australian* of 12 October 1991 which published this 'fact', 'the chilling find was made by a local veterinarian'. The (anonymous) vet caught the piranhas and put them in with his own pet fish. 'He realised something was wrong when he found fragments of his other fish floating on the surface.'

Despite the age of this legend, it hangs around. An American collection of urban legends published in 2000 was titled *Alligators in the Sewers*. It makes regular appearances on the Internet and as an occasional newspaper filler when the journos have fallen asleep, or have their tongues planted firmly in their cheeks.

In 2000 it all appeared to come horribly true one late November weekend in Sydney. As reported in the *Sydney Morning Herald* of 28 November, a builder in the suburb of Alexandria discovered an American alligator-snapping turtle lumbering through a culvert. The exotic beast, not yet fully grown, was over 50cm long and weighed around 25kg. A native of the south-eastern United States, alligator snappers can grow to 80kg. How did the turtle get there?

Back in 1979 a number of alligator-snapping turtles were stolen from the Australian Reptile Park. It was speculated that this was the origin of the turtle. Then again, just like alligators in the sewers, it may also have been an unwanted pet dumped by a bored or alarmed owner.

THE BOTTLES ARE STILL ROUND THE BED

Not exactly cryptozoology, perhaps, but certainly a weird belief about animal behaviour, **The Bottles are Still Round the Bed** is still there. The basis of this was first established by Bill Scott who noticed half-filled bottles of water littering gardens, nature strips and other grassy spots. Apparently, those who prepared the bottles and left them so strategically located were motivated by the belief that these devices deterred dogs from gracing the grass with their excreta.

Explanations vary as to why this should stop the neighbourhood pets from crapping on your garden. Some say that, to dogs, the half-filled bottles look like the droppings of other dogs and thus, being territorial, they shy away. Another explanation is that dogs will not defecate where there is fresh water, as they know this will pollute their drinking water.

A variety of methods are recommended for efficacious use of the bottles: they must be clear, only half full, sometimes partly buried, sometimes standing up.

Scott tenaciously traced the probable origins of this one to the USA, where the practice seems to have been around since at least the 1960s. Jan Brunvand reported the practice as being rampant across New Zealand in 1988 and has documented it in America from at least the early 1980s. The bottles appeared first in Australia during the mid-1980s and have been discussed and recommended or debunked in newspapers, magazines and on radio shows around the country.

There is apparently no scientific or any other basis for this one, and I thought it would have faded away by now. But no, they're still there. Up and down the streets of the nation you can still see them, lying on their sides or standing upright on their futile guard duty, glass or plastic bottles of water usually surrounded by piles of doggy poo.

8

DON'T BE MYTH-TAKEN: BUSTING URBAN LEGENDS

WHAT CAN WE do to protect ourselves from urban legends? How can we know when we are being 'had', especially if the person who is telling us the story believes it to be true? We need to know how to distinguish a 'true' urban legend from the many other stories that float about via the media, the Internet and by word of mouth.

In the last year or so I have heard or read a number of stories that have the hallmarks of urban legendry. They include the story of the girl who died after an operation to remove a hairball from her stomach, as discussed in Chapter 3. Then there was the captivating story of the young Japanese women who were wearing underwire bras during an electrical storm, and were subsequently struck by lightning. Instant annihilation in a big blue flash. Some versions of this tale claim that it was just their clothing that was blown away. Take your pick. Either might be true or both might be false.

So, how can a person separate the spurious from the factual?

[URBAN LEGEND – BUSTING]

If you suspect that you are being told an urban legend, Jan Brunvand's PPQ test (Polite, Persistent Questioning, mentioned in the Introduction to this book) is a useful one. But be ready to cop flak from the teller because you're treading on *their* myths.

Increasingly though, urban legends are coming to us from non-verbal sources, including the mass media, the micro-media of small-distribution newsletters, notices and flyers and especially through the Internet and by e-mail. In these circumstances it is not possible to apply the PPQ technique. But that doesn't mean that we need to be defenceless. There are some positive and useful steps you can take to bust urban legends before they bust you.

The first thing to be aware of is the topics, themes and situations that are typical of urban legends. Rumours and legend scares can arise whenever and wherever circumstances are appropriate. History, though, reveals that certain situations are more likely than others to generate these outbreaks, such as:

Wars
    Active duty
    Homefront
    Propaganda
    Espionage

Disasters
    Natural (for example, floods, fires, quakes)
    Human (for example, massacres, stock-market crashes)

Riots
    Race
    Food

Community Panics
    Serial murders/rapes
    Satanism
    Abductions
    Hysterias ('June Bug')
    Paedophilia panics
    Drugs
    Halloween
    Home invasions (for example, burglary, rape, etc)

Financial
    Stock exchange and general financial rumours
    Bank runs

Commercial
    Food products
    Cosmetics and toiletries
    High-profile product brands and corporate images

Occupational
Student pre-examination rumours
Workplace rumours
Professional

Political
Resignations
Scandals

Celebrities
Sex lives
Health
Careers

These are major danger spots for urban legend scares. They are not the only ones, of course and you might like to have a look at the following A-Z of urban legend themes and topics that appear in this book, and in the earlier *Granny on the Roofrack*.

As well as knowing the sorts of things urban legends are likely to be about and/or the circumstances in which you're likely to encounter them, you need to know how to detect them.

[URBAN LEGEND DETECTION]

The pervasive anecdotes of anxiety and fear we call 'urban legends' or 'urban myths' seem to be increasing in number, occurrence and sophistication. As many of the examples in this book demonstrate, urban legends have been given a powerful impetus by the developing technologies of the

Internet and e-mail. Such stories are generally presented, whether orally or in written and electronic forms as true, often leading to widespread alarm and panic. One of the paradoxes surrounding these forms is that even though we may be aware of their existence, urban legends often have the ability to mutate and sneak up on our healthy scepticism or our not-so-healthy gullibility in a new version.

For some serious legend busting, here's a more detailed version of the 'Pocket Legend-Detection Kit' included in the Introduction. Just apply the following tests to any intriguing new anecdotes heard or read:

1. Ask for the source of the information. Who told the teller? Who told them? Ask for names, dates, places, sources. Did the person who told them actually see it themselves?

Urban myths are often told and retold as first-person or eyewitness experiences. Even when the teller does not seek to claim that he or she was directly involved, the structure of the narrative and the expectations of the genre are such that personal involvement is almost always implied. A tactful probing as to whether or not the speaker was on the spot is a vital first step in establishing the reliability of the information being conveyed.

2. If you hear or read the story again, from whatever source, do any of the details vary, even a little, especially with regard to where and when it is supposed to have happened?

Informal transmission of information — orally or electronically — is inherently unstable and liable to variation, even over short periods of time and across short distances. Passing on the tale will almost always cause variations in some of the details. Such inconsistencies are a good indication that you are hearing or reading a 'factoid'. Unfortunately, one of the paradoxes of factoids is that the more they are told the greater their credibility, regardless of their authenticity. The simple act of transmission and of hearing and/or reading the same story from different sources imparts an air of credibility that is often difficult to debunk.

3. Does there seem to be an element of exaggeration and hyperbole in the telling?

For reasons that still remain essentially mysterious, human beings can rarely resist the temptation to 'out-tell' the previous teller of a tale. Fish must be bigger, burdens must be heavier, bosses harder, explosions louder, burglars bloodier, and so on. A good model to keep in mind here is the classic fishing tale of 'the one that got away' — the size of the lucky fish gets bigger with every telling.

4. What is the 'yuk factor'? Is there an unusual or odd element about the tale? Is it bizarre, grisly, macabre or horrific?

This is closely related to exaggeration, but it is important to be aware of the 'yuk factor' as a distinctive characteristic of many urban legends. Some typical topics and locations of urban legends are included in the list of Urban Legend Themes in the following section.

5. Is it logical and rational?

Can you really survive and function without both your kidneys, for instance? Can you actually fit a baby into the average microwave oven?

While there may be instances where something like these things have happened, they are few and far between, and almost always undocumented or poorly verified. The incidents that typically form the core of urban legends are highly improbable, and certainly could not occur with the frequency suggested by the wide diffusion of stories that recount them.

6. Does it have a story-like structure?

This usually involves a beginning, middle and ending, a character or characters, things that happen to them or that they do and some sort of resolution or ending, often a 'sting in the tail' of the story.

Under the influence of modern communications technology, urban legends are becoming increasingly elaborate, with multi-event and multi-character narratives becoming more common. They are also starting to develop 'consequences' as part of the story. For example, in the **Kid(ney)napping** legend discussed previously, it is usually claimed that as a consequence of the epidemic of organ stealing, the emergency operating theatres of local hospitals are jam-packed with de-kidneyed young men. This has the effect of increasing the anxiety level inherent in the story, also a typical feature of consequences. However, from the point of view of the sceptic, such elaborate narratives and consequences are usually reliable indicators of urban legendry in action.

7. Despite having a story-like structure, few if any urban legends feature named protagonists. It is always 'This guy...' or 'My sister knows a woman who...' Once again, lack of specificity is a sure sign of delusion at work.

8. Does there seem to be some kind of moral or warning attached to the tale?

One of the primary functions of these modern narratives seems to be to raise our awareness of the *possibility* of the things they describe happening to us, or to those we love. As fables, even parables, they seek to alert us to possibilities we would otherwise prefer not to think about. So, if a story heard or read on e-mail seems to point out a moral, it may well be an urban myth.

[AN EXAMPLE]

Here is an example of how this detection method might be applied to an urban legend event. I've used a real-life telling of the 'Hold Everything' legend here, but you can do the same to any suspect e-mails that come your way.

A friend of a friend went out for a meal at a local restaurant 'recently'.

The woman ordered a well-done steak. When the meal arrived, it was so rare that she sent it back for further cooking. The steak returned, cooked to her satisfaction but as the steak was very large she was unable to finish it and requested a 'doggy bag' for the remainder of the steak.

By the time she reached home she was not feeling very well and became suspicious that there was something wrong with the steak. The next day she sent it 'for analysis'. When the results came back, they said that the steak was covered with the semen of four men. The matter will go to court shortly.

This is a typical 'contamination legend', as discussed in Chapter 4. The woman who told the story believed it to be true, even when confronted with the fairly polite scepticism of one or two of those present. Applying the steps outlined above to this tale, we can quickly determine the likelihood of its being a legend:

1. Who told the story to the teller?

In this case it was a female 'friend' who was told about it by her 'friend'. This is the classic 'friend-of-a-friend' source of urban legends.

2. Other tellings of the tale.

It was quickly and easily ascertained that others had heard the story earlier that week, though they were vague on the details. Again, this is typical of urban legends.

3. Elements of exaggeration.

The detail of four different semens making up the 'sauce' is a clear suggestion of the size of 'the one that got away' syndrome.

4. The 'Yuk Factor'.

Plenty of this here!

5. Logic and rationality.

Would four men ejaculate on the steak? Why wasn't one sufficient?

How would four men find the time, not to mention the opportunity, to masturbate and ejaculate onto a steak in the middle of a busy restaurant kitchen?

Unpleasant though this tale is, there is no reason why semen should make one ill. (Though this obviously does not apply to the hepatitis and AIDS versions of the tale.)

How would an average person know how to go about having the steak 'analysed', and what would it be analysed for?

6. Story structure.

This legend has a definite beginning, middle and end. The initial situation of the meal in the restaurant followed by the development of the underdone steak, its return, the woman's illness, subsequent suspicions and their confirmation by scientific testing which reveals the plot element previously hidden — that the kitchen staff were so incensed by the woman returning her underdone steak that they decided to get their revenge by adulterating the food.

7. Absence of named protagonists.

No-one who appears in this story is actually named.

8. Moral or warning.

The clear intention of this tale is to warn others against the dangers of eating in this particular restaurant and, more broadly perhaps, others like it.

This story and its telling, then, scores extremely high on the scepticism scale. We can be 100 per cent sure that it is an urban legend. It is therefore most unlikely to be true, and those who believe it and tell it to others are being deluded.

These quick, practical tests can be easily applied to any suspected 'factoids' that you hear. Not all will register such an impressive level of spuriousness. But it is easy to rapidly satisfy yourself — and others — that what is being purveyed as 'true', is almost certainly not, no matter how much the teller is likely to insist that it *is* true, because they heard it from a friend-of-a-friend.

Readers interested in these applied aspects of nonsense studies might like to have a look at the 'baloney kit' contained in the late Carl Sagan's *The Demon-Haunted World*, a compendium of rhetorical and other strategies of double-speak, illogicality and sheer nonsense. Michael Shermer includes a similarly useful discussion in his *Why People Believe Weird Things: Pseudoscience, Superstition, and Other Confusions of our Time* (Freeman, NY, 1997), while many of the popular science works of Stephen Jay Gould also deal with popular misconceptions and myths.

URBAN LEGEND THEMES

While there are a great many urban legends, most deal with a limited number of recurring themes and topics. Legends contained in *Granny on the Roofrack* are also included here, marked with an asterisk*. Many legends have more than a single theme or moral, so the same legend may appear under different categories.

ABDUCTION

ALL GONE!
SHANGHAIED TO CANBERRA*
THE BABY SNATCHER*
THE BABY-NAPPING BIRD*
THE CASTRATED BOY*
THE KIDNAPPED DAUGHTER*
WHITE SLAVERS IN THE LOO*

AIDS

AIDS MARY*
AIDS MEMOIR*
THE AIDS COFFIN*
THE ORIGINS OF AIDS*

ANIMALS

'ABC's
ALLIGATORS IN THE SEWERS*
BACKFIRE!
BUNNY BUSINESS*
BUNYIPS, YOWIES AND YARAMAS
DOG'S DINNER*
MAG WHEELS
PET MEAT*
POOR MOGGY!*
PRESSED CHIHUAHUA*
THE BABY-NAPPING BIRD*
THE BLOODY BURGLAR*
THE CANE TOAD HIGH
THE CAT IN THE BAG
THE COOKED CAT
THE FAITHFUL HOUND*
THE FROZEN CHOOK AT THE CHECKOUT*
THE LITTLE RED HEN: AN UPDATE*
THE LOADED RABBIT*
THE PEANUT BUTTER SURPRISE
THE WELL-DRESSED ROO*

BABIES AND CHILDREN

A PLEASANT CHANGE*
ALL GONE!
BLUE STAR ACID*
GOING BY THE NUMBERS
REDEMPTION BY POP-TOP*
REDEMPTION BY POSTCARD*
SHANGHAIED TO CANBERRA*
SLOW DANCE
THE BABY IN THE MICROWAVE*
THE BABY SNATCHER*
THE BABY-NAPPING BIRD*
THE BLACKOUT BABIES
THE CASTRATED BOY*
THE FAITHFUL HOUND*
THE KIDNAPPED DAUGHTER*
THE TAPEWORM*
THE USED SYRINGES

TRICK OR TREAT?*
TUPPERWARE TOPS
WHITE SLAVERS IN THE LOO*

BELIEFS

REDEMPTION BY POP-TOP*
REDEMPTION BY POSTCARD*
SLOW DANCE
THE BOTTLES ARE STILL ROUND THE BED*
THE GREAT BARCODE BEAST AND OTHER NUMBERS
THE ORIGINS OF AIDS*
TRICK OR TREAT?*

BODILY PENETRATIONS
AND INFESTATIONS

AN EARWIG ON THE BRAIN*
BACKFIRE!
BODILY FLUIDS
FIZZY COLON*
FRIENDLY AND GAY
FULL UP
KID(NEY)NAPPING*
PHOTOGRAPHIC EVIDENCE*
THE BALI SPIDERS*
THE BOUFFANT HAIRDO*
THE FATAL HAIRBALL
THE FROZEN CHOOK AT THE CHECKOUT*
THE GREAT KIDNEY PANIC OF '98
THE REDBACKS IN THE DREADLOCKS*
THE TAPEWORM*
TRAVEL BUGS

BODY PARTS

A BIG CRUNCH IN THE MOUTH
AN EARWIG ON THE BRAIN*
ASHES TO ASHES*
BODILY FLUIDS
DOG'S DINNER
FIZZY COLON*
KID(NEY)NAPPING*
REDBACKS IN THE DREADLOCKS*

BURGLARS

CONTAMINATION

DEATH

DOG'S DINNER*
GRANNY ON THE ROOFRACK*
PET MEAT*
POOR MOGGY!*
PRESSED CHIHUAHUA*
REDEMPTION BY POP-TOP*
REDEMPTION BY POSTCARD*
ROAD MOVES
SLOW DANCE
THE AIDS COFFIN*
THE BABY IN THE MICROWAVE*
THE CAT IN THE BAG
THE COOKED CAT
THE CORPSE ON THE CAR ROOF*
THE DEATH CAR*
THE DIVORCEE'S REVENGE*
THE EXPLODING DUNNY*
THE FAITHFUL HOUND*
THE FATAL HAIRBALL
THE HEAD*
THE HEADLESS BIKIE*
THE LOADED RABBIT*
THE ORIGINS OF AIDS*
THE REDBACKS IN THE DREADLOCKS*
THE RESURRECTED CAT*
THE TAPEWORM*

DRUGS

BLUE STAR ACID*
FRIENDLY AND GAY
THE BABY IN THE MICROWAVE*
THE CANE TOAD HIGH
THE DRUG TRAFFICKER'S TAX DEDUCTION
THE USED SYRINGES

EMBARRASSMENT

A FART IN THE DARK*
AN EVEN BIGGER SURPRISE*
ASHES TO ASHES*
BACKFIRE!
BODILY FLUIDS
BUNNY BUSINESS*

CAUGHT AT THE CHECKOUT*
FIZZY COLON*
FRIENDLY AND GAY
FULL UP
PEA–PEAS–PEAS *
PISS OFF, REG!*
SURPRISE IN THE SHOWER*
THE COPULATING COUPLE*
THE DINNER PARTY*
THE EXPLODING DUNNY*
THE FROZEN CHOOK AT THE CHECKOUT*
THE NAKED CARAVANNER*
THE PEANUT BUTTER SURPRISE*
THE PIGGYBACKING BABY-SITTERS*
THE SURPRISE PARTY*
THE X-RATED HONEYMOON*
TIME FOR A KIT-KAT*

FOREIGNNESS

ALLIGATORS IN THE SEWERS*
DOG'S DINNER*
KID(NEY)NAPPING*
ORDURE IN THE COURT
SHANGHAIED TO CANBERRA*
THE BALI SPIDERS*
THE GREAT KIDNEY PANIC OF '98
TRAVEL BUGS
TRAVELLERS' CAUTION
WHITE SLAVERS IN THE LOO*

HOAXES

'ABC's
ACT NOW!!!
BLUE STAR ACID*
BUNYIPS, YOWIES AND YARAMAS
BURGLARY ALERT
DIHYDROGEN MONOXIDE (DHMO)
ELECTRONIC WORMS
HELL OF A WELL
IT TAKES GUTS TO SAY 'JESUS'
GOING BY THE NUMBERS
PISS OFF, REG!*

REDEMPTION BY POP-TOP*
REDEMPTION BY POSTCARD*
SLOW DANCE
THE GNOMES ARE BACK!*
TRICK OR TREAT?*

HORRIBLE ACCIDENTS

A BIG CRUNCH IN THE MOUTH
ASHES TO ASHES*
BACKFIRE!
BUNNY BUSINESS*
FIZZY COLON*
MAG WHEELS
PET MEAT*
POOR MOGGY!*
PRESSED CHIHUAHUA*
REDBACKS IN THE DREADLOCKS*
THE AERIAL SCUBA DIVER (Introduction)
THE BABY IN THE MICROWAVE*
THE BALI SPIDERS*
THE CAT IN THE BAG
THE COOKED CAT
THE DINNER PARTY*
THE EXPLODING DUNNY*
THE HEADLESS BIKIE*
THE LOADED RABBIT*
THE SEVERED FINGERS*
TRAVEL BUGS

INSECTS

AN EARWIG ON THE BRAIN*
REDBACKS IN THE DREADLOCKS*
THE BALI SPIDERS*
THE BOUFFANT HAIRDO*

MISTAKES AND MISHAPS

A BIG CRUNCH IN THE MOUTH
A PLEASANT CHANGE*
AN EARWIG ON THE BRAIN*
ASHES TO ASHES*
BACKFIRE!
BUNNY BUSINESS*

FIZZY COLON*
FULL UP
MAG WHEELS
PET MEAT*
POOR MOGGY!*
PRESSED CHIHUAHUA*
SURPRISE IN THE SHOWER*
THE BABY IN THE MICROWAVE*
THE BLACKOUT BABIES
THE BLOODY BURGLAR*
THE CAT IN THE BAG
THE CONCRETE CAR*
THE COOKED CAT
THE COPULATING COUPLE*
THE EXPLODING DUNNY*
THE FAITHFUL HOUND*
THE FALSE TEETH*
THE FROZEN CHOOK AT THE CHECKOUT*
THE LOADED RABBIT*
THE NAKED CARAVANNER*
THE RESURRECTED CAT*
THE 747 HAS EVERYTHING*
THE TAPEWORM*
TIME FOR A KIT-KAT*
TUPPERWARE TOPS

MORAL PANICS

AIDS MARY*
AIDS MEMOIR*
BLUE STAR ACID*
KID(NEY)NAPPING*
THE AIDS COFFIN*
THE CASTRATED BOY*
THE GREAT BARCODE BEAST AND OTHER NUMBERS
THE GREAT KIDNEY PANIC OF '98
THE MILLENNIUM BUG
THE ORIGINS OF AIDS*
THE USED SYRINGES

NARROW ESCAPES

A HAIRY HITCHHIKER*
BACKFIRE!

FIZZY COLON*
GIRLS!!! BEWARE!!!
IS ANYBODY HOME?
SHANGHAIED TO CANBERRA*
THE BABY SNATCHER*
THE HEAD*
THE HOOK*
THE KIDNAPPED DAUGHTER*
THE KILLER IN THE BACK SEAT*
THE LADY WITH HAIRY ARMS*
WHITE SLAVERS IN THE LOO*

NUDITY

AN EVEN BIGGER SURPRISE*
IS ANYBODY HOME?*
SURPRISE IN THE SHOWER*
THE DINNER PARTY*
THE NAKED CARAVANNER*
THE PEANUT BUTTER SURPRISE*
THE PIGGYBACKING BABY-SITTERS*
THE SURPRISE PARTY*
THE X-RATED HONEYMOON*

PETS

ALLIGATORS IN THE SEWERS*
BACKFIRE!
BUNNY BUSINESS*
DOG'S DINNER*
MAG WHEELS
PET MEAT*
POOR MOGGY*
PRESSED CHIHUAHUA*
THE BABY-NAPPING BIRD*
THE BLOODY BURGLAR*
THE BOTTLES ARE STILL ROUND THE BED'*
THE CAT IN THE BAG
THE COOKED CAT
THE DINNER PARTY*
THE FAITHFUL HOUND*
THE RESURRECTED CAT*

REDEMPTION

REDEMPTION BY POP-TOP*
REDEMPTION BY POSTCARD*
SLOW DANCE

REVENGE

A PLEASANT CHANGE*
ORDURE IN THE COURT
THE AIRLINE STEWARD'S REVENGE*
THE ALFALFA REVENGE*
THE CONCRETE CAR*
THE DIVORCEE'S REVENGE*
THE FALSE TEETH*
THE LOADED RABBIT*
THE SEVERED FINGERS*
THE SUPERGLUE REVENGE*
THE WEDDING PHOTOS
THE WELL-DRESSED ROO*

SATAN

HELL OF A WELL
THE GREAT BARCODE BEAST AND OTHER NUMBERS

SCAMS AND CONS

CAUGHT AT THE CHECKOUT*
LOST PROPERTY, PROPERTY LOST
THE WIZARDS OF WEALTH
TICKETS TO A SHOW*
WATCH OUT FOR JENNIFER URICH

SECURITY

A HAIRY HITCHHIKER*
A HOLIDAY WIN*
ALL GONE!
BURGLARY ALERT
FRIENDLY AND GAY
GIRLS!!! BEWARE!!!
IS ANYBODY HOME?
LOST PROPERTY, PROPERTY LOST

PHOTOGRAPHIC EVIDENCE*
SHANGHAIED TO CANBERRA*
TALKING FEAR
THE BABY SNATCHER*
THE BLOODY BURGLAR*
THE CASTRATED BOY*
THE FAITHFUL HOUND*
THE HOOK*
THE KIDNAPPED DAUGHTER*
THE KILLER IN THE BACK SEAT*
THE LADY WITH HAIRY ARMS*
THE MILLENNIUM BUG
THE X-RATED HONEYMOON*
TICKETS TO A SHOW*
TRICK OR TREAT?*
WHITE SLAVERS IN THE LOO*

SEX

A BIG CRUNCH IN THE MOUTH
AIDS MEMOIR*
AN EVEN BIGGER SURPRISE*
BACKFIRE!
FIZZY COLON*
FRIENDLY AND GAY
FULL UP
IS ANYBODY HOME?
KID(NEY)NAPPING*
SHANGHAIED TO CANBERRA*
SURPRISE IN THE SHOWER*
THE AIDS COFFIN*
THE AIRLINE STEWARD'S REVENGE*
THE ALFALFA REVENGE*
THE BLACKOUT BABIES
THE CONCRETE CAR*
THE COPULATING COUPLE*
THE DINNER PARTY*
THE DIVORCEE'S REVENGE*
THE GREAT KIDNEY PANIC OF '98
THE KIDNAPPED DAUGHTER*
THE NAKED CARAVANNER*
THE ORIGINS OF AIDS*
THE PEANUT BUTTER SURPRISE*
THE PIGGYBACKING BABY-SITTERS*

THE SUPERGLUE REVENGE*
THE SURPRISE PARTY*
THE WEDDING PHOTOS
THE X-RATED HONEYMOON*
WHITE SLAVERS IN THE LOO*

SHOPPING

ALL GONE!
CAUGHT AT THE CHECKOUT*
SEVERAL GROSS ASSORTED CONTAMINATION RUMOURS
SHANGHAIED TO CANBERRA*
THE BABY SNATCHER*
THE CASTRATED BOY*
THE FROZEN CHOOK AT THE CHECKOUT*
THE GREAT BARCODE BEAST AND OTHER NUMBERS
THE KIDNAPPED DAUGHTER*
THE KILLER IN THE BACK SEAT*
THE LADY WITH HAIRY ARMS*
TIME FOR A KIT-KAT*
WHITE SLAVERS IN THE LOO*

STUPIDITY

A HOLIDAY WIN*
AIDS MEMOIR*
AN EVEN BIGGER SURPRISE*
ASHES TO ASHES*
CAUGHT AT THE CHECKOUT*
THE FROZEN CHOOK AT THE CHECKOUT*
THE LOADED RABBIT*
THE SURPRISE PARTY*
TICKETS TO A SHOW*
TUPPERWARE TOPS

SUPERNATURAL

HELL OF A WELL
THE DEATH CAR*
THE GREAT BARCODE BEAST AND OTHER NUMBERS
THE PHANTOM HITCHHIKER*

TECHNOLOGY

ACT NOW!!!
ELECTRONIC WORMS
HELL OF A WELL
IT TAKES GUTS TO SAY 'JESUS'
MAG WHEELS
PHOTOGRAPHIC EVIDENCE*
TELSTRA AND OPTUS 90#
THE BABY IN THE MICROWAVE*
THE COOKED CAT*
THE MILLENNIUM BUG
THE MINISTER'S TELECARD
THE 747 HAS EVERYTHING*
THE X-RATED HONEYMOON*

VANISHING

GRANNY ON THE ROOFRACK*
THE CORPSE ON THE CAR ROOF*
THE PHANTOM HITCHHIKER*

WORMS

(Real ones; see under TECHNOLOGY for the virtual variety)
SEVERAL GROSS ASSORTED CONTAMINATION RUMOURS
THE TAPEWORM*

MORE ABOUT URBAN LEGENDS

The legends and related materials collected in this book, and in my previous collection *Granny on the Roofrack* (1995) are, or were, all circulating in Australia at some stage in oral form, in print or on the Internet — more usually in any combination of these. It is a characteristic of modern folklore in the information age that it can, and often does, exist in forms other than the traditional word of mouth. Nevertheless, it operates in much the same way, and with the same results as it always has. The Malays call rumours 'news on the wind', a fitting description of the speed and spread that characterises them, as well as legend and associated misinformation. Increasingly, the wind is an electronic one that blows almost instantaneously through the computer networks of the globe.

While some legends fade away they never seem to die completely, and can always be resurrected when the circumstances are right, or wrong, either in their original form or in some mutation appropriate to the new situation. New legends also appear from time to time, though as further research often reveals, these can frequently be traced to earlier origins. Even if the legend has not existed before in its current shape, then at least one or some of the motifs on which it turns may be drawn from the international and mostly ancient stock of folktales.

Formerly the kind of ephemeral and apparently trivial anecdotes and oddities that characterise urban legends and other informal communications were given short shrift by just about everyone, most folklorists included. But there has been a growing realisation that these forms of modern dread, delusion and occasional black humour are important, if ambiguous, expressions of the information era. Certainly they are being subjected to serious and prolonged study by researchers from many disciplines. There is now an extensive body of writing about urban legends in several languages, ranging from the heavily theoretical and academic, to the lightly entertaining.

Best-known to the general public, perhaps, are the many works of the American folklorist Jan Harold Brunvand, who wrote *The Vanishing Hitchhiker* (Norton, New York, 1981) a book that built on the earlier work of English writer Rodney Dale, *The Tumour in the Whale* (Duckworth, London, 1978) and initiated a continuing and growing popular interest in these modern tales told around the world. Brunvand's most recent contributions include *Too Good to be True: The Colossal Book of Urban Legends* (Norton, New York/London, 1999) and *The Truth Never Stands in the Way of a Good Story* (University of Illinois

Press, Urbana/Chicago, 2000*)*. He is currently compiling an encyclopaedia of urban legends.

There are also collections and discussions of urban legends in Swedish, German, Dutch, Spanish and French, as well as a growing number in English, including a number of South African anthologies by Arthur Goldstuck. Details of Goldstuck's books are published on his website (see below). English folklorist Paul Smith has published two collections of urban legends, *The Book of Nasty Legends* (Routledge & Kegan Paul, London, 1983) and *The Book of Nastier Legends* (Routledge & Kegan Paul, London, 1986). A recent British study of story-telling among adolescents, Michael Wilson's *Performance and Practice: Oral Narrative Traditions Among Teenagers in Britain and Ireland* (Ashgate Publishing, Aldershot, 1997) also contains a good deal of information on the subject.

There is an annual journal devoted to urban legends and related matters. Titled *Contemporary Legend*, it is published by the International Society for Contemporary Legend Research, a British/North American organisation that also publishes the newsletter *Foaftale News*. This organisation holds annual conferences and has published the proceedings in a series of books, titled *Perspectives on Contemporary Legend* (Sheffield Academic Press, Sheffield).

Many folklore journals and magazines carry articles about urban legends, including *Australian Folklore*, which has published relevant articles by Australian and overseas folklorists, including Mark Moravec, Bill Scott and Gwenda Davey.

The collection and discussion of urban legends in Australia was instigated by folklorist and author Bill Scott, who was on the trail of these tantalising tales back in the 1960s. Since then he has published a number of works dealing with legends, including *The Long and the Short and the Tall* (Western Plains Publishers, Sydney, 1985) and *Pelicans and Chihuahuas: and Other Urban Legends* (University of Queensland Press, Brisbane, 1996). Amanda Bishop published a collection of Australian legends in *The Gucci Kangaroo* (Australasian Publishers, Sydney, 1988) and Ron Edwards included a selection of the urban legends he has collected in his *Fred's Crab and Other Bush Yarns* (Rams Skull Press, Kuranda, 1990). Gwenda Davey has written about Australian urban legends in *Overland* and for the *National Library of Australia* magazine.

I have written about urban legends and related topics in various ways, including *Great Australian Urban Myths* (Angus & Robertson, Sydney, 1995), *The Bare Fax* (Angus & Robertson, Sydney, 1996), 'Careless Whispers', *The Australian*, June 12, 1998, p. 32, 'Funny Business' (*The Australian*, July 23, 1998, p. 30 and 'Mall Stories' (*Independent Monthly*, May, 1994).

Some other disciplines also have an interest in urban legendry, including social psychologists, sociologists and those who study the closely-related topic of rumours. Works in these fields include:

Fine, G., *Manufacturing Tales: Sex and Money in Contemporary Legends* (University of Kentucky Press, Knoxville, 1992)

Koenig, W., *Rumor in the Marketplace: The Social Psychology of Commercial Hearsay*, (Auburn House, London, 1985)

Pratkanis, A. and Aronson, E., *Age of Propaganda: The Everyday Use and Abuse of Persuasion* (New York, 1992)

Rosnow, R. & Fine, G., *Rumor and Gossip: The Social Psychology of Hearsay* (Elsevier, New York/Oxford/Amsterdam, 1976)

Victor, J.S., *Satanic Panic: The Creation of a Contemporary Legend* (Open Court, Chicago, 1993)

Not related specifically to urban legends are two books that highlight the ease with which the sorts of delusions and fears on which they are based spread, and also provide useful corrective techniques. These are:

Sagan, C., *The Demon-Haunted World: Science as a Candle in the Dark* (Random House, New York, 1995);

Shermer, M., *Why People Believe Weird Things: Pseudoscience, Superstition, and Other Confusions of Our Time* (W. H. Freeman & Co., New York, 1997).

There is also considerable interest in the urban legend from researchers in the field of memetics, briefly discussed in the Introduction. Some relevant books are:

Dawkins, R., *The Selfish Gene* (Oxford University Press, New York, 1976);

Lynch, A., *Thought Contagion: How Belief Spreads Through Society: The New Science of Memes* (Basic Books, New York, 1998);

Blackmore, S., *The Meme Machine* (Oxford University Press, New York, 1999).

In addition to these printed work, there are a number of Internet sites and user groups dedicated to urban legends. Active at the time of going to press, these include:

The San Fernando Valley Folklore Society's Urban Legends Reference Pages: www.snopes.com/

David Emery's About.com Urban Legends: www.websearch.about.com/

An Australian site, the Urban Legends Research Centre: www.ulrc.com.au/

Arthur Goldstuck's urban legend site, 'Legends from a Small Country': www.legends.org.za/arthur/

And finally, the earliest Internet site legend site, still going strong: alt.folklore.urban

Flies in the Ointment: Medical Quacks, Quirks and Oddities

From Dr Jim Leavesley and Dr George Biro, authors of *What Killed Jane Austen?* and *How Isaac Newton Lost His Marbles* comes *Flies in the Ointment: Medical Quacks, Quirks and Oddities,* their third rollicking and sometimes grisly collection of medical and celebrity whodunnits and whatdunnits.

* What really killed Elvis Presley?
* Why did Dr Summerlin paint black patches onto white mice?
* How did Dr Michael Servetus come to be burnt as a heretic?
* What was Boswell's social disease?
* Why was Rasputin so indestructible?
* How did Mozart meet his demise?

Written with Leavesley and Biro's trademark clinical flair and knack for diagnosing the truth, *Flies in the Ointment: Medical Quacks, Quirks and Oddities* reveals the often dark and seamy side of human nature and uncovers the important details the forensic pathologists missed! It's a prescription for intrigue, mystery and fun.

ISBN 0 7322 6933 4